A Journey to Faith . . . Catholic Mass aboard a Korean Conflict troop ship bound for Hawaii.

# Near to My Heart

## An American Dream

William K. Nasser, M.D.

Nasco Publishing Company
Indianapolis

Book Project by
Hawthorne Publishing
15601 Oak Road
Carmel, IN 46033

ISBN: 0-9729991-0-8

Additional copies of this book may be obtained from St. Vincent Hospital Foundation, Indianapolis, Indiana.

This book is typeset in larger than normal type at the request of the author for the benefit of those whose eyes may appreciate larger type.

# Dedication

An American dream cannot be fulfilled without parents. Therefore, I would like to dedicate this book to my parents, Toufaike Kaleel Nasser (T.K.) and Maude Nasser. In many ways they continued to support me financially, emotionally, and with love and affection. And above all else they taught me honesty, integrity, and a sense of family values which I have attempted to maintain.

I would also like to thank my two sisters Beverly Radez and Dolores Polifroni for their loving support.

# Foreword

Dr. William K. Nasser (Dr. Bill) was born during the Great Depression in a decaying neighborhood in Terre Haute, Indiana. The neighborhood was a diverse ethnic mix of immigrants from all over Europe and the Middle East.

Dr. Bill's father, Toufaike Kaleel Nasser, known throughout his life as T.K., established the neighborhood's main grocery store. It was the social center for local housewives who shopped each day and caught up on neighborhood news. Mothers took their preschool children with them and these children often played in the store while mom shopped and gossiped. I met Dr. Bill in this manner—a skinny little four-year-old with one of his father's aprons rolled up and tied around him as he tried to wait on customers. Thus, began a friendship that has lasted for sixty-five years and can go on for ten times that long if God will let it.

T.K. took great pride in his only son, and Bill could observe his dad as Godfather to us all, extending credit to anyone who needed it or delivering groceries to those who could no longer walk to the store. With one of the few cars in the neighborhood, T.K. was there to take the sick to the doctor or bail one of us out of lock-up. If you couldn't talk to your own father, you talked to T.K. Eventually, a large group of neighborhood boys, "our gang," was formed with the Nasser store as its headquarters. Camping, hunting and sand lot sports all had their beginnings at, or in front of, the Nasser store. At one time or another every boy in the neighborhood was employed at the Nasser grocery, an opportunity that contributed to much needed family income for most of us.

Bill grew up with considerable admiration for his father and, as a result, was to develop great insight as to what makes a society function. He emerged as a leader and organizer. He was not a very good student; none of us were. Neither was he a long-range planner; he was a "doer." Bill organized the building of our clubhouse and, when needed, a teen social center for the whole town, among many other things.

By the standards of our neighborhood, the Nassers were a wealthy family. They had a car, indoor plumbing, a live-in housekeeper and clothes and groceries without budgeting for them. It was only later Bill came to realize that he also lived just outside the poverty zone. To be successful, the store required that all members of the family participated: Bill's mother, Maude, and two sisters, Beverly and Dolores.

It was the neighborhood that made the family's modest income seem high. That and T.K.'s generous and giving nature in dealing with community and family. T.K. Nasser sold groceries on credit to anyone in the community who needed it and never once referred a non-paying customer to a collection agency or sought legal help. In later years, as Dr. Bill built his small cardiology practice into a huge heart facility, he would also never seek legal help in collecting his patient's bills. Bill was to emulate his father's generosity throughout his life and it became part of his nationwide image.

While in college, Bill was drafted for the Korean Conflict and was soon in combat 8,000 miles from home.

Something touched Bill while he was in the trenches. I have been a sailor for most of my life and they say, "No one stands at the helm of a small boat with a force 10 blowing 1,000 miles from shore and doesn't believe in God." It is likely that enemy fire has the same effect because Bill returned as a deeply religious man. This, too, has stayed with him throughout his life.

In this next episode of his life, I believe that God continued to play an important role.

When Bill had open-heart surgery at Georgetown University Medical Center at the age of twenty-six, this type of surgery had a very high risk. With his father, mother and wife, Wanda standing by on that Friday morning realizing every patient who had undergone the surgery that week had died on the operating table, Bill submitted to an anesthetic which he believed would probably last forever.

He woke up with a new life, to become the world's longest living recipient of a new aortic heart valve, a record he has maintained for forty-two years. That experience, more than anything else, pointed Bill towards cardiology as a career beginning his lifelong ambition to help save lives through improved procedures in heart care.

You will have to read on for the story of this extraordinary man's career and his pursuit of the American Dream. Bill has received almost every award his profession, his university or his state can offer. His highest awards, however, come from seeing his sons, Tony and Tom, follow him in the medical profession: Tony as a cardiologist with the clinic Bill founded and Tom as a successful endodontist.

There is now a house full of grandchildren as well presided over by his wife, Wanda, the best doctor's wife anyone could imagine and still beautiful after forty-four years with this spirited and dedicated man.

Donald E. Moffitt
Chairman of the Board
CNF, Inc. (formerly Consolidated Freightways)

# Foreword

There are very few people on our planet who understand the physiological, psychological and overall makeup of human beings like Dr. William K. Nasser. As you would expect, Dr. Nasser's new book about his life, *Near To My Heart :An American Dream* is a touching, thoughtful and genuine autobiography of a man who has given so much to the development of modern cardiology. The text describes the life of a man who has encountered death as a soldier, young medical student, young practicing physician and a near drowning. Despite these close calls with death, Dr. Nasser emerged as a stronger, more passionate and disciplined individual whose desire to live and provide care for others is far beyond that of the normal human being.

*Near To My Heart* describes the makeup of the man and the physician who is one of America's true pioneers in cardiovascular medicine. Additionally, the text describes an entrepreneur who learned from personal experiences as a young man to care about people, as well as the science of medicine. It is through Dr. Nasser's personal challenges and experience with life-threatening events that he has been able to apply a strong entrepreneurial spirit to the practice of cardiology. This ultimately led to the creation of one of the largest cardiology groups in the United States.

In 1989, I had the personal privilege of meeting Dr. Nasser in Indianapolis to talk about the future direction of cardiology and the possibilities of furthering his group. He agreed to engage our firm to assist him in meeting the challenges of the 1990s including managed care, increased organization requirements and application of innovation. One of my fondest memories of Dr. Nasser was his statement to patients and other physicians that 'Happiness is Clean Coronaries.' Without a doubt, Dr. Nasser has contributed more to modern day cardiology than any other physician or health care executive I have ever met. *Near To My Heart* aptly describes the challenges that Dr. Nasser encountered and the obstacles he overcame throughout his life.

I hope you will enjoy reading this book and will be inspired by Dr. Nasser's insightful text that communicates two very thought-provoking mesages: "Life is very precious, don't take it for granted" and "Life should be planned but must be lived daily in order to meet tomorrow's challenges."

John O. Goodman
President
John Goodman & Associates, Inc.
Las Vegas, Nevada

# ACKNOWLEDGMENTS

I would like to express my gratitude to Donald E. Moffitt and John O. Goodman for writing the forewords of this book.

Words cannot express the gratitude I have for my loving wife, Wanda of forty-four years. She has been a devoted and loyal friend and has carefully edited every word of this text. Without her support I could never have pursued my dreams. She allowed me to focus on my passion of medicine and took up the role as Mom and Dad in my building years.

My three children, Teresa, Tom, and Tony have been extremely supportive of me, allowing me the opportunity to pursue my goals.

I sincerely thank my five grandchildren for giving me great joy and pleasure: William (B. T.) and Anthony Tanoos and Taylor K., Tiah K. and William K. (Billy) Nasser II. I hope this book will serve as a legacy of inspiration for them as they pursue the American dreams that are *near to their hearts*.

I am very appreciative of Carol Kourany, to whom I owe so much for her invaluable editing of this manuscript. She was also very instrumental for providing the insight and reasons for me to begin my autobiography. Her husband Edgar has also assisted me during our travels.

I would like to express my sincere thanks to Donna Margason, my administrative assistant, in the preparation of this document.

Dr. Duke Haddad and Dr. Bob King made invaluable contributions to this book.

I would also like to thank Bob Carlson for his excellent questions and responses during the recording of this book.

Nancy and Art Baxter played an incredible role in assisting me with the preparation of this book.

St. Vincent Hospital Foundation, St. Vincent Children's Hospital and the St. George Orthodox Church in Terre Haute were very inspirational to me.

Dr. Harris B Shumacker has been a friend for many years and helped guide my professional life and I am forever indebted to him for this.

My family, friends and professional colleagues were very helpful to me in building a cardiology organization that continues to deliver modern up-to-date health care as it relates to the heart.

*The fulfillment of the American Dream requires being in the right place at the right time, maintaining an achievable goal through motivation, persistence in your commitment, a positive attitude and remaining focused. It is also good to have a certain amount of fortune called "Luck."*

*These are the basic ingredients in life necessary to achieve success. Life is a journey—not a destination.*

William K. Nasser, M.D.

## Chapter One

# Beginnings at Terre Haute

Wise men have said that in every life there is one defining moment or time, a time which marks and changes a life and out of which flow all the other moments and days. My defining moment must have been in 1954, when I was in the US Army, on a troop ship heading for active duty in the Korean War.

During the two weeks we were on that stinking, crowded ship, I was unhappy, sick to my stomach, and somewhat angry that I was in the predicament of having been drafted and on my way to the shooting action of the war.

I met a chaplain who in the course of conversation asked me a provocative question: "Nasser, what would you like to do with your life when you get out?" "You know, I really don't know," I answered. He grew thoughtful. "Nasser, when you find yourself in life, then you'll know what you're all about—and then what you want to do." Struck by what this chaplain told me, I decided to take his advice and find out what I was all about— and then to do something worthwhile. It did not come to me immediately what that something would be, but over the time I was in Korea, I began to believe that although nobody in my family or circle of friends was a doctor, I wanted to go into medicine.

Perhaps the one defining moment in my life was really two, because when the war was over and we were sent to Hawaii, there in the barracks in Honolulu, I noticed that one soldier, an Irishman, got up early Sunday morning, made his bed neatly, and went off somewhere—presumably to church. Although my father had taken us to the Syrian Orthodox Church, it could not be said that we followed any religious tradition. I'm not quite sure why, but I finally asked this soldier if I could go to church with him. I was changed during that period and decided to become a Catholic and devote my life to others. Again, medicine seemed logical to fulfill that desire to serve.

What seemed like an unachievable goal for the son of an immigrant, who had been drifting through college before he was drafted, making Cs at Indiana State University, with little money for school, became a life-long passion. The road was long, with many byways, but the truth is it grew wider all the time until today, when I still work actively in a fulfilling career as senior adviser to one of the largest corporate cardiology practices in the world. That path, however, had begun before the moment of truth on the way to Korea. It began when a baby was born June 3, 1933 in Terre Haute, Indiana.

My father had immigrated from Damascus in the 1920s. He came to what seemed like an unlikely area for a middle-Eastern community. Terre Haute was a coal mining, meat-packing, railroad town on the banks of the Wabash River. Farmers came in from all of mid-central Indiana and Illinois, from towns like Casey and Robinson, Illinois, and Sullivan and Farmersburg, Indiana. Located there at the Crossroads of America (US 40 and US 41), it was a bit notorious; anything seemed to go there, including political corruption and prostitution, at least in the 1920s and 1930s. Still, it had its intellectual side; Indiana State Teacher's College, now Indiana State University, was located there, with about 4,000 students at the time.

Terre Haute's history had been marked with some incidents of intolerance from the time of Copperhead sentiment during the Civil War through the Ku Klux Klan days following World War I. Still, America was the land of opportunity, and several Syrian families had come, generally going into merchandising on a small scale. There were fifty-two Nasser grocery stores in Terre Haute at one time during this period.

Nasser is a common name in Syria, like Smith in America today. My father, Toufaike Kaleel Nasser (known to all as T.K), had left two of his sisters behind when he came; it was his paternal uncle who welcomed him to Terre Haute and introduced him to my mother, Maude. Maude's last name was (not related) Nasser also! She was only sixteen years old when she entered the arranged marriage. She never completed high school, but went to work in the family store and took care of the children who were born.

My maternal grandfather, George Nasser, Mom's dad, came to America around 1900 and eventually settled in Fort Wayne, then moved to Terre Haute. He met and married Ziney Nasser, my grandmother. It was in Terre Haute that my mother was born and grew up.

Both my mother and my father worked in the store. T. K. Nasser and Son had a complete line of groceries in a mom-and-pop sort of atmosphere. We lived behind the store: parents, two sisters, and me.

My father was a savvy, wise man of the "old country" stock. He convinced the local wholesale grocery supplier Hulman & Company to supply him with $300 worth of merchandise on credit to start the grocery store. Hulman delivered corn and beans and everything else people picked up from the shelves. Folks in the neighborhood had heard a neighborhood store was opening, and I guess they wanted canned goods, meats and fresh vegetables, because by the end of the day all the stock was gone and my father was counting his cash.

My father spoke Arabic and broken English, as did my maternal grandparents. My mother spoke both Arabic and English. I chose the English and never mastered Arabic, to my regret. My sisters Beverly and Dolores turned out to be good students at Deming grade school in Terre Haute. I didn't; grade school bored me. Occasionally I was called into the principal's office for some sort of minor disciplinary infraction, like reading comic books in class. Maybe playing a little hooky. Any of us called into that office would have to bend over and be whopped with a paddle.

Soon I was headed for Gerstmeyer Technical High School, long gone now, which was the high school in our poor neighborhood. Gerstmeyer was a vocational school. At that time I was preparing to enter some trade, and spent my time in the auto shop class learning how to repair a car. I learned to arc weld, and I also took print shop and a typing class.

I was interested in athletics, but never seemed to be any good at it. I made the B football team, but I guess the coach took a look at skinny, not-too-broad–or-tall me and decided I was never going to bring fame to the school in football.

What I was really excelling in at the time was social behavior. That was a course I could get As in. I helped form the Canteen Club in the late 1940s in Terre Haute so that teenagers from several Terre Haute high schools could get to know each other. We had our first get-together at the Coca-Cola plant, with lots of kids involved. There'd be a live band, not musically excellent probably but providing jumping music for the jitterbugging we were doing or a D.J. playing 45s of the Ink Spots or Perry Como. Soft drinks for refreshments.

There were teachers there, sitting at tables in the back of the room and applauding the group spirit which encouraged town pride. I know we all cheered for any Terre Haute high school at the state basketball sectionals and regionals. They were all our friends.

I really should admit I didn't appreciate my Syrian heritage during those years. There were all the drawbacks of discrimination connected to it. My skin was a little darker, my nose a little longer than those of the local Vigo County crop of kids. When I was about ten years old and began to ride the bus downtown, I'd have to go to the back of the bus. My father wanted to be a Mason; they wouldn't take him. None of our Arab-speaking community could get into the Terre Haute Country Club. One incident happened when I was a freshman in high school. I was interested in a freshman girl, and my gang of buddies and I used to walk everywhere around town, so I walked to my "girlfriend's" house. Her parents peered out of the windows. They wouldn't let any of us on the porch because we were "of other ethnic backgrounds than theirs."

Perhaps they'd heard stories of our gang—exaggerated no doubt. We had built a small clubhouse on a vacant lot across the street from our house, and we played a little poker, tried a Camel cigarette or two, sampled a bottle of Muscatel wine perhaps. No connection to the gangs of today, with the drugs and violence we hear about. We probably thought we were Hoosier versions of the "Bowery Boys" we saw in the local movie theaters.

Our wildest adventure would have been walking three or four miles to the old swimming hole in the heat of summer. Interestingly, those boys grew up to do interesting and successful jobs. Donald E. Moffitt is Chairman, President and CEO of the Board of Consolidated Freightways, the largest trucking company in the world. Bill Britton is now a retired coach and high school principal; Nick Sereno is a retired policeman, and Nick Perrelle is a retired truck driver. All of these members of the old gang, now grandparents, still live in Terre Haute except for Don who lives in California. So I guess being influenced by the Bowery Boys didn't hurt our gang too much.

I began Indiana State in 1951. Disinterestedly, I listened to lectures on William Wordsworth in Freshman English and Sigmund Freud in Introduction to Psychology. In the afternoons I helped my father in the grocery store, as I had since I was about ten years old. That was more interesting, because I could get to know and interact with people. We scurried around reaching on the shelves for "general merchandise." The store carried a little bit of everything. Since those first days when Hulman & Company had sent over a few cans of corn and beans the stock had grown substantially. We had staple groceries, meats and beer and wine as well as dry goods: women's dresses and lingerie, jeans, shoes, hardware, equipment for potbellied and kitchen stoves, and so forth.

My business-oriented mind was ever active and I loved sales best of all. My dad left town for a vacation, and I had a "Boss is Gone" sale. And I must have invented the "loss leader" sale in the early fifties in Terre Haute. I thought about attracting customers, and one day this came to me. We couldn't make money on Coca-Cola because the wholesale price was so high, so why not sell it on sale, lose a little in that sale and "bring 'em in" for all their other shopping needs for the weekend! Could be considerable profit in stock-up buying. We bought Cokes, six bottles for 24 cents. Why not sell them for six for 19? Nobody else was doing anything like that, and Cokes were a special treat (not the everyday item they are today) for most folks. With their nice little bottles sitting chilled in the Frigidaire, they added fun to the weekend radio college football games or Jack Benny show.

We sold three hundred cases in the first week. We also sold almost every other item in the store, including a store record of fifty-two pairs of shoes in one day. So we made money on the stock-ups and lost some on the Coca-Cola. I sold bacon for 19 cents a pound when it cost us about a quarter a pound wholesale. We sold tons of bacon. The hogs of central Indiana had to strain themselves to meet our demand. And people crowded the store, demanding the fruits and vegetables and dry goods and flour and sugar of this wonderful store. I was quite successful when I managed part time, though I think I must have made my father's head spin at times. Still, he had to double the size of the store about this time.

And I'd make little hand bills on 8x11 sheets of paper, featuring bread for 8 cents a loaf, bacon for 19 cents a pound. I'd get a group of young guys together who needed to make a couple of dollars and we'd plot out certain neighborhoods to cover with the hand bills. The couriers would deliver our enticing advertisements to the front doors of our target neighborhoods. When I was in charge of T.K. Nasser and Son General Merchandise Store, Saturday and Sunday mornings were absolutely busier than hell. Clearly I did have entrepreneurial blood in me.

The picture of my father dominates my remembrances of those days. My old gang members, who get together every now and then, recall him as a wise man, an influence on all the boys who knew him. Italians, Lithuanians, Poles, Hungarian kids: the gang met at our house in bad weather, and often these friends were employed as part-time workers in the store. So they got to know T.K. He was referred to as "The Mayor of Hunkey Town."

We were all from relatively poor families who had to work exceptionally hard, and my father had a kind of practical philosophy about how to make things work. Primary to that philosophy was working for your money. Sedentary, a little overweight, with high blood pressure and smoking Camel cigarettes all of his life, he didn't take good care of himself physically, but he knew what it took to live.

Total honesty was one of his main precepts. One day when I was in pre-med and had graduated to manager of the store, a man came in wanting to sell us bluejeans at a dollar a pair. "Yes," I said excitedly, visualizing the profit we could earn from selling those jeans. My father pulled me aside. "No, son. Slow down. We don't know where this man got those jeans. They may be 'hot goods.' We don't want to get involved with that." "Oh," I said, nodding slowly, realizing that what he said was probably right. You can't take the risk of dishonest behavior in any business, and I learned that from him. "Keep your family name good," he always counseled.

I got to know the local physcian, Dr. William Baldridge, a competent doctor and nice guy who came to the house in those days with his little black bag to inoculate us children against smallpox and diphtheria and to treat us for the usual complaints.

This he did in between delivering babies, treating the elderly in their last illnesses and performing surgery.

When I was about seventeen, I developed severe abdominal pain, and my father, in his old country way, said, "You just need a good flushing out." He gave me something—castor oil or an enema—but it didn't help. Dr. Baldridge had to be called and admitted me to the hospital with peritonitis. My appendix had ruptured. The laxative had aggravated it.

Dr. Baldridge did the surgery, but peritonitis is life-threatening, and I lay there, between life and death. My dad, being the old country man he was, grew distraught seeing his only son, the boy who was going to carry on the family name, fading away in the hospital bed. He went home that night and came back at 6 AM dressed in an overcoat and a fedora, looking like some gangster. Then he pulled a gun on Dr. Baldridge. "If he dies, you die with him." Needless to say the family practitioner called in a surgeon to help, and I recovered and lived to tell this tale. The doctors teased him about that for years, but my dad meant it seriously.

But my experiences with the doctor didn't at all make me want to go into the medical profession at that time. No, that was for later. My profession was already laid out for me. I was going into store-keeping, even if it meant my dad had to buy a big store for me to keep me interested. And, when I was drafted and knew I had to go to Korea, he nodded and said, in that chewed-up English he spoke until the day he died, "After you get back . . . after you get back, you will have your own store."

My maternal grandparents George and Ziney Nasser had many relatives in both Syria and Terre Haute.

My parents Maude and T.K. Nasser were married young and had three children. I was the eldest.

Toufaike Kaleel (T. K.) Nasser in the style of a business gentleman of the early 1930s.

T. K. and Maude built a successful grocery and general merchandise store in Terre Haute, Indiana.

My Boy Scout pals (front row, l-r) are Bill Barnhart, Nick Sereno; (back row, l-r) Don Moffitt and myself.

| | |
|---|---|
| Coffee Nasser's Special | lb. **18¢** |
| Navy Beans | No. **1** Mich. **5** lbs. **14¢** |
| Corn Country Gentlemen | **3** No. **2** cans **25¢** |
| Jolly Jell Gelatine Dessert Anv Flavors | **4** Pkges. **19¢** |
| Super Suds | large **19¢** small **10¢** |
| Octagon Powder | **3** Pkges **10¢** |
| Big Peet Soap | Bar **4¢** |
| Palmolive Soap | Bar **5¢** |
| Octagon Granules | large pkge **19¢** |
| Palmolive Beads | pkge **5¢** |

**PUREX**
**Qt**
**Bottle**
**15c**

| | |
|---|---|
| Matches or Salt | **3 - 5¢** boxes **10¢** |

**Flour**

| | |
|---|---|
| **5 lb.s** | **19c** |
| **10 lbs.** | **35c** |
| **54 lbs.** | **66c** |

United Patent

| | |
|---|---|
| VIGOLA FLOUR | 24 lb. **77¢** |
| Dog Food | 3 cans **17¢** |
| Dill Pickles | Qt. can ea. **15¢** |
| Soda Crackers | 2 lb. box **15¢** |

One of the grocery store's special promotions in June, 1935.

Gerstmeyer Stage Club in 1951. I'm second from right in the front row.

## Chapter Two

# Korea

Korea was just about as far from Terre Haute as you can get—at least culturally. I served from 1953 to 1955. For basic training I went to Fort Knox in Kentucky, then Camp Chaffee in Arkansas and after a few other stops to Fort Lewis, Washington. We shipped out from Seattle.

When we got off the boat, these eighteen-year-olds from all over the country saw people who looked really different from us, and we saw low, flat houses, flat rice fields, and, of course, a huge army camp.

It had taken two weeks to cross the Pacific. I have been through open heart surgery more than once, have had a liver transplant, but I think that two weeks on the ocean, with winds and high waves, was the sickest two weeks of my life. A toilet on a boat is called a head, and I can understand why when I think of that vomitous voyage. I figured out why they call the boat toilet the "head." Every commode in the head had a head in it constantly. The entire boat stank. I lost fifteen pounds.

One reason for that was because we stood to eat our meals, all 3,000 of us. The eating trays were all connected, without separation. If someone "tossed his cookies" at the eating table, everybody's tray was affected. Sleep was hard to come by; bunks were stacked eight or nine high.

But now we were here, near Seoul and going through the routine things the soldiers supporting the United Nation's mission against North Korea had to do—get clothing and assignments for location and tents and prepare to support the soldiers at the front. I found out I was assigned to a machine gun squad. I was to fire the machine gun, and the assistant gunner would carry it. That, at least, was something; the machine gun weighed twenty to thirty pounds. The gunner himself carried only the tripod, a trifling weight. I had learned to dismantle and mantle a machine gun about as fast as anyone could, and it was at this time I was promoted to corporal.

So on the march I carried that tripod, my pack and a Browning Automatic Rifle, a big rifle, that thing you see soldiers salute with, present arms and so forth.

It was cold and rainy and, of course, the life of a soldier is never pleasant, even behind the front lines. You do your washing, drinking and shaving out of a helmet, the beds are freezing cold, the food is palatable, nothing more. The men at the front, completing the war there in 1955, were experiencing far worse.

Fourteenth Infantry, US Army. We took guard duty. We made twenty-mile marches with full packs. Every hour a ten-minute break. We collapsed on those breaks, and I was so tired I would sleep nine minutes. We were machines, doing what we were told, no questions asked. Our position was called Camp Casey. We supported the front nearby.

I suppose I have a sensitive nose. As we marched past those rice paddies and villages, I noticed the most awful odor, everywhere. Korea is perhaps the most beautiful area I've seen, with green-clad hills and fields and distant mountains. Its beauty for me rivaled pictures I'd seen of Norway or Sweden. It can fill your eyes and heart, but in this case it also filled our noses. What was the constant sewer odor? Koreans, it seems, used human excrement instead of cattle dung to fertilize their fields. The rice paddies stank, and these small-bodied people would stand patiently all day long, planting and taking care of rice plants without seeming to notice.

I was surprised to notice that during the time I visited the latrine, one of twenty or so Army ration latrines set up in a row, that there would be a whiff of air come in below me. If you turned around you could see a little Korean "honey dipper" collecting the human excrement and putting it in a bucket. Two buckets or bags of fertilizer would be carried on the end of poles by hundreds of these farm workers all over the roads. It was a new cultural experience.

We began to get to know the Korean people. Boys we called boysan would clean up the tents; women, mamasan, would come in to help with laundry. We were strongly warned against having any romantic relationships with the women. We were told that there was a ninety percent chance of venereal disease if we entered into a sexual relationship.

Some men believed they would be the one in ten who did not have trouble, and sought out the local women. The percentages caught up with them, and they had to be treated with penicillin. After they'd returned to the slum brothels a few times, the disease would be refractory to treatment, and they would have permanent damage to their health in later years.

We were at the front lines, and although the war was winding down, action was continuing near us. We see movies of the war, *M.A.S.H.* for instance, with soldiers rushing everywhere. It wasn't like that. Soldiers would be in a bunker covered with sandbags. Every once in a while a soldier would stick his head up and fire a bullet at somebody in an enemy bunker.

The fighting was going on at the 38th Parallel separating North and South Korea, only a couple of miles from us, and so hundreds of wounded soldiers were being brought back, especially in the first two weeks after we arrived. Trucks or jeeps would bring them into the field hospital, where they could be treated or shipped out for special surgery. Some were terribly wounded, disfigured, with arms and legs blown off from land mines or from bombs or injuries during special all-out advances.

What I most remember personally is the noise—the terrible noise of that machine gun I had to take care of. It shot with such a deafening roar that it brought me to tears a couple of times. They did not for some reason supply us with earplugs, so we just had to cover our ears or tough it out. I think if I had been through the entire war near one of those big machine guns, I would have gone deaf.

Today I chuckle when I occasionally see war movies to see how technically ignorant of war the script writers are. Burt Lancaster holds an air-cooled machine gun in the movie *From Here to Eternity,* which is now having a second round of popularity in video. That's absolutely impossible; one of those guns is so hot when firing that it will burn the flesh right off your hand. Today they cool the barrel with water, a big improvement over the air-cooled models of our time.

I made many friends; we dug foxholes together, the eternal occupation of soldiers who don't have anything else to do. Then we filled them up again. There were good times, too. We bathed in the river and visited the coffee houses. Soon the truce was declared and the war wound down. We stayed six months, and then they sent us to Hawaii, because the war was over.

Hawaii seemed like paradise after Korea. We were quartered at Schofield Barracks. Some aspects of it were like a country club, with a swimming pool and an Olympic-size diving platform. Many of us would go into Honolulu when we could get a pass, some to visit the prostitutes along Hotel Street. We could go to Waikiki Beach and sun right in front of the Royal Hawaiian Hotel. This we accomplished by paying ten cents at the military beach facility, and then climbing the fence to sun with the plutocrats in front of the Royal Hawaiian Hotel.

I had grown up a bit since I left Terre Haute, and I began to have some insights. At that hotel were old folks who couldn't come down and join us on the beach. They were up there in their hotel rooms staring out the windows. I thought, here I am, I can enjoy it but can't afford it and here they are: they can afford it but can't enjoy it.

We learned to surf a little; we drank the good Pearl beer popular in the Islands. At Don the Beachcomber's we watched the hula girls, ate pu pu appetizers and drank zombies. "Don't drink more than two," the popular lore went. There were eight kinds of alcohol in a zombie. One night I had considerably more than two zombies and the next morning I could see that the advice was right.

It was here, of course, that I had time to reflect on the troop ship chaplain's questions about my life. After I went to mass with that Irishman from the barracks, I became a Catholic and have been, I hope, a devoted one ever since. I suppose what I liked about it was that it gave you rigorous rules to live by and frowned, in the name of God, on misbehavior and sin. Maybe I needed that. I took Catechism courses and began to try at least to lead a Christian life. And it came to me that I could help others with medicine. I could justify my existence in the world and do some good while I was here. I could become a doctor. The idea was just forming; I would pursue it when I got back to the States.

While all this was going on, I was giving some thought to a girl I'd met on leave, during my state-side army experience. She wasn't exactly the "girl I left behind me," yet—but I was thinking about her. Wanda had lived in Brazil, Indiana, and was a secretary for Shell Oil in Terre Haute. We'd met at the Steak 'n Shake, a local meeting place, at 8$^{th}$ and Wabash in Terre Haute when I was there with friends, as she was. We'd had dates; she was personable, unselfish and cute.

I was honorably discharged in 1955, headed home and then went to Indiana State as soon as I could to continue my education, with my new direction firmly in mind by now.

I sat in the office of the dean of students. "I'd like to take a pre-med course," I told him. He went to the file cabinet to get my transcript. Then he started laughing. "Look at this record, Nasser," he said. "You don't have any Ds or Fs, but neither do you have As or Bs. You're a C student. You're not smart enough to be a doctor."

I began to cry, to actually weep with disappointment and frustration, right there in the dean's office. The man looked at me with amazement, and backpedaled a bit. "All right, Nasser, I'll prove to you that you aren't smart enough. You'll see it yourself. I'll sign you up for the pre-med course."

And that was the beginning of a long road to the present.

My "ocean voyage" wasn't always rough.

Doing what soldiers have done for centuries—digging.

It didn't take long to build some muscle...

... particularly if you were horsing around with those 30-caliber machine guns near the front lines in Korea, 1954.

But Army life wasn't without some R&R to relieve the more dangerous times in Korea in 1954.

Hawaii and Schofield Barracks were a welcome stop over on the way home in 1954.

Waikiki Beach was great for all of us soldiers on our way back home. That's me second from left really "cooling it."

There wasn't much use for this Korean money, except to save as souvenirs and mementos.

## Chapter Three

# Plans for the Future

I had become very religious at this point. I told my father that my new Catholicism was very deep indeed, and that I was even considering becoming a priest. He would not hear of it and, of course, I, as the only son of an old-country man, listened attentively. "I want you to continue the family name. Have grandchildren. I want to leave a strong heritage behind when I go. No priesthood for you. You just go into the grocery business, like the rest of your family."

He saw I wasn't headed that way, so he looked for ways to re-direct me. "You're such a good salesman," he told me. He remembered the loss leaders on Coca-Cola and bacon. "Here—let's think about this. I'll buy you a supermarket."

But no, I stood my ground and entered the courses the dean of students at Indiana State signed me up for. And they were doozies. He had said he wanted to show me I wasn't smart enough to enter medicine, and so he put me in Algebra II, Advanced Chemistry, Advanced Zoology, and Physics. The problem was I hadn't had Algebra I, Beginning Chemistry, Zoology or Physics. Sink or swim, so I determined to stroke out with determination. What else could I do?

I sat there in those classes with those young boys and scratched my head. What was this all about? But then it began to make sense, and since I had greatly heightened concentration and a strong goal in mind, and a native interest in these things anyway, things began to click.

Believe it or not, working as hard as I had ever worked in

my life, I finished that first semester of advanced courses with all As. Then I continued with the beginning levels of these advanced courses and, needless to say, I earned As in these, too. What motivation will do for you!

I finished the next three years of college with a 4-point out of 4. When you put that together with 2 years of C, 2-point, you get a 3.3 to 3.4 GPA. And that was just borderline for admittance to medical school.

I wanted to be a doctor, but it wasn't going to be easy. I applied to Indiana University School of Medicine and was named an alternate; that is, if somebody already accepted and declined to attend, I could be considered.

But it did seem a bit of a long shot, and I waited and worried and prayed. That summer I decided to audit a course in Neuroanatomy—no grades to be given to me. I loved it and did so well that the doctor teaching the class said, "Nasser, you're going to make a fine physician."

"Sir, I need to tell you I'm not admitted yet." He was astonished and assured me I had a good chance of getting in. It was the next day, two weeks before school was to start, I received word that someone had declined, and I would be accepted. It was one of the most wonderful days of my life.

By now Wanda and I had been going together for quite a while, but both of us wanted to be sure that the life of a doctor's wife was the right thing for her. I told Wanda frankly that medicine was a jealous mistress and that there would be many times when I would have to put it first in my life. She understood that she would be taking on the management of the home and family, that she would be doing major guiding of our children when they came. But we were truly in love and she agreed to marry me understanding that her life would be challenging. My passion for medicine had become obvious by this time and was dominating me, as it would for the rest of my life.

I went through the first year of medical school in

Bloomington, under the system they had then, which included a year on the main campus and three years at the medical center in Indianapolis.

Wanda and I were married on December 23, 1958, during my second year in med school, when I moved to Indianapolis. She gave up her job in Terre Haute and took a job as a medical secretary in the Psychiatry Department at the med center. They offered insurance, and she asked me if I wanted to take out health insurance as a part of the institution's plan. "No," I told her, "I've never been sick in my life." "Well, I've got Blue Cross-Blue Shield and it doesn't cost any more to add you. Mind if I do that?" I told her it was okay if it didn't cost anything, but that I wouldn't need insurance. Was I wrong!

The GI Bill helped to defray some of the expenses of medical school. One hundred forty students made up our class. Classes were stimulating, and it seemed the answer to a dream—and a prayer.

We settled into a thirty-two foot trailer in Little Eagle Trailer Park on West Michigan Street where I'd been living for a few months.

Our trailer took about fifteen seconds to walk through. Still, it had everything in it we needed: living room, kitchen, shower, and bedroom. The only problem was that we as newlyweds had a roommate in that trailer. It seems that I had invited a classmate who had no place to live to set up a bachelor pad in the trailer with me. Wanda suggested that when we married it would obviously be time for him to move out, but I couldn't just set him out on the street. I'd promised him he'd have a place to live for a year.

And so the three of us coexisted in that trailer until finally he did move out, as our first child was on the way. That day Wanda joyously set his things outside the trailer and claimed it as her own. We were happy and I was in seventh heaven, heading towards the grand goal I'd set. Classes continued to go well;

friendships which have lasted to this day were formed. On November 14, 1959 Teresa was born and joined us in the trailer.

One friendship that was particularly interesting began for me in 1958 when I introduced myself to two freshmen medical students named Ed and Oscar Kourany. "You look foreign," I said. "My name is Bill Nasser." "You look foreign, too," they replied. They were identical twins from Panama, and Wanda and I cultivated a friendship with these young men and their wives. At the same time I met Jean Mercho, who was a surgical resident at General Hospital in Indianapolis (now Wishard). I also struck up a friendship with Dr. John Chalian, who was chairman of the Maxillofacial Prosthodontics Department at the IU School of Dentistry and his wife Zee. Through all these years we have remained friends.

The next year, when I was a junior in medical school, I began experiencing night sweats. At first they didn't seem severe, but they increased in intensity, so that I was getting up a couple times a night to change my pajamas. "You need to see the doctor at the med center," Wanda said.

The problem was, when I went in to describe this nighttime fever, it would have passed. My temperature was normal; all tests they ran, with blood work included, showed no problem.

After six weeks of feeling terrible at night and working through class and lab work during the day at the med school, I began to be frustrated. "What's the matter with me?" I asked, and one doctor I was consulting said, "You are surely experiencing anxiety attacks. I'd like to send you to a psychiatrist."

I began visiting the psychiatrist, and he sat there, peering at me over his spectacles and asking embarrassing questions. "Do you like men better than women?" "Are you anxious about your marriage?" and so forth. After four sessions of his trying to fish around for problems that didn't exist, and the mysterious night sweats continuing, I said in exasperation, "Doc, I wish I had some physical problem we could pinpoint. It would be easier to cure than this."

Wanda was now helping me change pajamas three or four times a night. "You've got to visit another doctor," she insisted. I went to see one of the genuine stalwarts of the Med Center, Dr. Glenn W. Irwin, Jr., who later became Dean of the School of Medicine and also Chancellor of IUPUI (Indiana University-Purdue University at Indianapolis).

Dr. Irwin asked me about the psychiatrist's visits and the continuing problem and asked, "What do you think is wrong with you?"

I shrugged. "I'm having anxiety reactions?"

"Well, maybe you are, but there's something else wrong with you. I'm ordering blood cultures." First of all, they discovered I had a heart murmur. And when they put me in the hospital, the blood cultures tested positive on six occasions. I had a streptococcal infection—infective endocarditis. It was very serious. As we progressed, Dr. Irwin discovered I had other symptoms: an Osler node, which means you have small microemboli at the tips of your fingers. I also had what are called splinter hemorrhages, little hemorrhages in fingernails. We don't see them any more in cardiology, because they are diagnosed earlier in the patient's history. But all of these things pointed to the fact that I had a heart valve infection—infective endocarditis of the aortic valve, which was end-stage.

Where did this infection come from? Usually one sees this problem after surgery. It usually occurs on an abnormal valve, either mitral or aortic. But I had not had surgery in the recent past.

They treated me with antibiotics, and I grew some better. The problem did not go away, however, but grew worse.

Dr. John B. Hickam, Chairman of the Department of Internal Medicine asked to see Wanda and me on a Thursday afternoon, the very day I completed my senior year of medical school. "Bill," he said, "You have a leak in your aortic valve and a marked enlargement of your heart, and I would estimate that you have approximately two months to live. Surgery might help." By this time we were expecting our second child.

How could this have happened to me? By the time I had been through all of those tests, and growing progressively worse through all the testing, I was finishing my last year in medical school. They had given me an accelerated program, finishing me three months early, because they knew I was seriously ill. So I was about to be graduated with a promising career, and I was told my life might end. To top it off, even though I had insurance which might cover most of the surgery, we didn't have the money to get to a hospital where surgery might be done.

Besides, the procedure I would need was open heart surgery, which was just beginning to be done, and was an extremely risky procedure. Very few were surviving during this time.

Dr. Hickam went through a list of the few surgeons in the country performing this type of heart procedure and gave me reasons for not going to see any of them. Then he said, "There is a doctor who is having some success with replacement of aortic valves at Georgetown University in Washington, D.C. His name is Dr. Charles Hufnagel. I've called him and you have an appointment for Saturday morning. You need to go there at once." Saturday morning was thirty-six hours away.

"Well, I may go out there, but I'm not going to have the surgery," I said emphatically.

Wanda and I frantically sought loans from relatives to fly out to Georgetown. My dad helped, and we were able to gather the money for the round-trip tickets. I bought $200 worth of travelers checks, which I did not need to use and have kept to this day. I've carried them around for the last forty-two years and feel they bring me good fortune. We got on the plane on Friday, and on Saturday morning I arrived at the door of Georgetown University Hospital.

"I can't do this," I thought, and began to turn around to leave. At that moment the door opened, and greeting me was Dr. John Hickam. "Come on in," he said. I was so impressed and relieved. An important man like Dr. Hickam had come to be with an insignificant medical student like me. I think the physicians at Georgetown were also impressed.

I was treated like a real doctor. I accompanied two giants in the medical profession on grand rounds that morning, Dr. Charles A. Hufnagel, Chief of Heart Surgery at Georgetown, and Dr. W. Proctor Harvey, Chief of Cardiology at Georgetown. In addition, they had me present my case in front of their Georgetown faculty, who were all in attendance at grand rounds. As I presented, everyone listened to me with stethophones hooked to the chair, so they could listen to the heart murmur.

Later, I was a little angry at all that had happened, and when Dr. Hufnagel began to confer with me about the surgery, I showed that anger. "What do I have to gain?" I asked, recalling how many people were dying on the operating table in cases like mine during this early phase of cardiac surgery. His comment came back, "What do you have to lose? You have only two months to live anyway!"

Well, that was true enough, I thought. So I resigned myself, with some small hope it might prove successful. The procedure was only six months old!

Families of the young people having open heart surgery gathered in the surgery waiting rooms. (Most of the people having open heart surgery in these early days were young.) Only one open heart procedure was done a day. Monday's patient, complete with family was there, Tuesday's, Wednesday's and Thursday's also, and then there was Bill Nasser and Wanda—and my parents, who had also flown in to stand by me as I became Friday's patient.

The patient who had surgery on Monday did not return. Tuesday's patient did not survive the surgery, either. Wednesday's patient did not make it, nor did Thursday's. And I was scheduled for Friday. The law of averages wasn't running my way. Still, it had to be done. I had last rites of the Catholic Church and they wheeled me away. And almost instantaneously, at least as it seemed to me, the surgery was complete and I had survived. Number One for the week.

The surgery had apparently gone well in Georgetown. They had found a congenital anomaly called bicuspid aortic valve—something I was born with. Yes, it had been infected and was failing fast. The skilled surgeon had used silicone silastic leaflets in open heart surgery, sewing three of them in to replace my valve. The decisions about placement and closing at that pioneering time were in the hands of the surgeon, who relied on his own instinct. The surgeons at Georgetown told me my valve seemed to be working. The doctors could not hear any murmurs of aortic insufficiency, a leaking aortic valve. But time would have to tell.

I recuperated for about ten days, and then I went home. I was headed for my internship. I had my heart set on being a heart surgeon myself. I wanted it in the worst way. My chairman, however, called me in and said, "Nasser, you aren't well enough to take a grueling residency in surgery. We want you to start out with an internship in internal medicine."

I was to have one year of internship, and then two years of residency, and I was ready for it. But now, as I was examined in Indianapolis, the physicians began to find the valve was leaking after all. The murmur that had been discovered during surgery increased; the valve was leaking increasingly. I was going to have to have it replaced sooner or later. In the meantime, I went on with the internship and the first year of residency in Indianapolis.

Months after my subsequent heart surgery, doctors found a draining sinus in my gums, an abscess. I had had to have incisions and drainage of the abcess, and they felt this infection was the original source for my infected heart valve.

In 1963 when I was a resident in internal medicine, I began to get into the practice of medicine outside the hospital. I was asked to do a *locum tenens*—replacement for a doctor while he was away, taking care of his patients. Was this a thing I should do I wondered while I was doing the residency? Consulting with my superiors, I found that it was permissible, so long as my malpractice insurance was in place.

I was standing in for Dr. Jay Reese, who had also been in the med school Class of 1961 with me, and had gone directly from school into the practice of general medicine in Martinsville. He could guarantee me $350 a week, and we could use the money for certain. Our first child, Teresa was four; Tom was two.

"How much do you make?" I queried. "Well, I'm more experienced than you are now, and I make about $600 a week."

"Wow! Do you think I could make that?"

"I don't think so. I don't think you have the skills for it." We'll see about that, I thought.

"Tell all the doctors in Martinsville that I'm willing to cover for any of them," I said. If I was going to do this, I might as well cover a lot of ground. The arrangement was that the first $350 I'd make would be mine, the next $250 would go to Jay's office expenses, nurse and so forth and anything beyond that would be mine.

I didn't know what to charge, but Jay said he'd analyze my treatments and charge appropriately when he came back from his trip.

Dr. Reese, it turned out, was a busy doctor and I spent my time visiting the hospital, getting to know all kinds of patients, delivering babies, relocating fractures that were not open, giving anesthesia, doing minor surgeries. I was the typical general practitioner of those days and I didn't get much sleep. I worked as much good medicine per hour as I possibly could.

When Dr. Reese returned from his vacation and calculated

my services, I received a check for—$3,000. In my first week of general practice. Dr. Reese scratched his head in amazement. I smiled. My annual salary at IU Medical Center for Residency was only $2,500.

For my part, I decided this moonlighting could be a lucrative thing. I didn't have to live the life of a poverty-stricken resident. I formed a little consortium of residents who would rotate in the Martinsville outpatient emergency department, and this arrangement went on for several years. I liked it; it gave me a variety of experience; I supplemented my income. So even when I had a cardiology fellowship and was in an advanced stage of my training, I was still helping babies come into the world. I believe it was the first time an actual emergency department medical situation had been set up at a hospital in Indiana.

Today, of course, emergency department physicians have to be board-certified. But in those days general practitioners covered emergency cases which came in on weekends, doing all that had to be done from Caesarian sections to gallbladder operations. What was really happening was that I was getting a lot of extra training. And I got good at medical diagnosis. As that Martinsville experience went on, I began doing consultations for other physicians, and then cardiology consultations, a field in which I was completing my training.

In 1964 I started my cardiology fellowship. They permitted me to spend three months at Georgetown University Hospital at Washington. D.C. mentoring with my heart surgeon Dr. Hufnagel, and my cardiologist, Dr. Harvey. The fellowship was stimulating, and it was rewarding to be working at a major cardiovascular center with two giants in the medical field. I will always be grateful for this part of my training.

When the two-year fellowship was over, I joined the staff of IU Med Center. Dr. Charles A. Fisch, the Chief of Cardiology, took me with him to Bloomington to hear him deliver a lecture and do some consults. As we went through the hospital at Bloomington, he was surprised to hear doctors in the halls saying, "Hi, Bill!" to me. "You seem to know everybody," Dr. Fisch said, surprised.

Here's what had happened. During all these years of moonlighting, I had come to know many physicians in Martinsville. I'd been working with them and eventually consulting. But Martinsville isn't very far from Bloomington, and when a urology specialist was needed, for instance, in Martinsville, someone from Bloomington would come up. So I knew many doctors in both towns by now and they began sending patient referrals to me at the IU Med Center in Indianapolis. It was the beginning of a way to practice medicine for me that was both efficient and rewarding. Go out of your way to earn trust from your colleagues in other towns in your state and they will provide you with patient referrals and provide economic stability for your career. Soon it was true that if a doctor had a patient with a heart problem, he'd send that patient to Nasser.

My Martinsville experience was the beginning of a statewide referral network that was a novelty in the state's medical practice, one which was soon functioning efficiently in cities like Martinsville, Terre Haute, Bloomington, and Elkhart all referring to me at the IU Medical Center.

I continued moonlighting. I thought I had to: my annual salary was $14,000 when I came to IU Med Center as an assistant professor of medicine and $20,000 six years later.

My responsibilities at the Medical Center included teaching, research and patient care. But my responsibilities for the patients grew as the referrals grew. I was sure I was onto a good thing. For instance, one of the people I trained with in my cardiology fellowship was Dr. Marvin E. Mishkin. No heart surgery was being done at the time in Elkhart, where he practiced, so he sent the Elkhart referrals to me. And before long other physicians from Elkhart were sending their patients to me. We are talking about valvular cases or congenital heart disease. Coronary artery disease treatment was a thing of the 1970s—still ahead of the time I'm describing.

We were still seeing cases of heart disease following rheumatic fever in those days, something we uncommonly see today in the United States. Today, antibiotics and prophylactic care taken during dental exams and inoculations prevent the awful complications from diseases like streptococcal infections resulting in rheumatic heart disease that we saw in the 60s.

Teresa at six months having breakfast with Dad in the trailer in Little Eagle Trailer Court, Indianapolis. I was a junior medical student.

## SOME HISTORY

### Open Heart Surgery

In 1948 Dr. Harris B Shumacker became the first Indianapolis surgeon to practice open heart surgery. Surgeons who did open heart were also performing other types of surgery: gallbladder, appendectomies in addition to the new discipline. In a short time heart surgery became a specialty.

To perform open heart surgery, a new type of machine had to be developed to allow the heart to be shut down and worked on during a procedure to correct a congenital heart problem or to correct a valve imperfection. The heart-lung machine had been developed in 1953 by Dr. John Gibbons in Philadelphia; seemingly a miracle of modern medicine much commented on at the time.

In 1960 the first mitral and aortic valve prosthesis was placed. Dr. Hufnagel developed the leaflet technique used at Georgetown Medical Center.

In 1967 Dr. Rene Favoloro, a surgeon from Argentina, did the first saphenous vein bypass for coronary heart disease at the Cleveland Clinic.

Catheterizations

In 1929 Dr. Werner Forssman did mirror image surgery, making an incision in his arm and threading a catheter up into his right atrium.

In 1945 Dr. André Cournand won the Nobel Prize in Medicine for developing modern catheterization technique: a catheter is put into the heart to measure pressure of the heart, diagnose and inject dye to trace the movement of fluid through the heart.

In the late 1950s two physicians, Dr. Mason Sones from Cleveland Clinic and Dr. Melvin Judkins from Portland, Oregon, developed coronary catheterization techniques

In the early 1960s Indiana University School of Medicine in Indianapolis was engaging in heart catheterizations and open heart surgery; by 1970 private hospitals began heart catheterization and open heart surgery, thus expanding the practice beyond the academic centers.

In 1961, when I was finishing med school with increasingly failing health, we met a new priest, Father George Rados, who had come to Terre Haute to serve the St. George Orthodox Church. Although both Wanda and I were practicing Catholics by this time, we were interested in meeting this fine young priest, who was serving our relatives' religious community. He had just graduated from the seminary, and both Wanda and I liked him immediately.

When Wanda and I were suddenly told that I needed to have heart surgery and we flew cross-country, that Friday in May of 1961, Father Rados left the church doors open day and night, so the Syrian community, Orthodox and non-Orthodox, could come to pray and light candles for my successful surgery and return to good health.

His letter sent after my successful surgery said, in part, "How beautiful it was to walk into the church and to find it illuminated with so many candles, to see the activity of people coming and going, offering prayers for your return to good health."

After Father Rados, many beloved priests have continued serving that community. Today's priest, Father Anthony Yazge, is presently leading the church in celebrating their seventy-fifth anniversary and planning for the building of a new Orthodox Church in Terre Haute. Father Yazge has continued to carry out the Orthodox ministry. He is very much loved by parishoners and citizens in the community as well as his wife and family. St. George Orthodox Church in Terre Haute will continue forever.The religious tradition goes on, as it has in my life.

And I had survived my surgery returning to practice medicine with a firm conviction that all those Terre Haute prayers were still following me, and I had quite a bit of work yet to do.

Later the family expanded. Bill, Wanda and Tony are in the first row and Teresa and Tom in the back.

## Chapter Four

# My Practice Takes Off on Its Own

In 1967 my aortic insufficiency had worsened to such a point that I needed another aortic valve replacement. This was done at the University of Alabama Medical Center in Birmingham by Dr. John A. Kirklin, a native of Muncie, Indiana, and graduate of Harvard Medical School. He had been Chief of Surgery at the Mayo Clinic in Rochester, Minnesota, and by this time I knew about the open heart surgeons in the country and wanted to have him perform my surgery.

That granddaddy of heart valves that I had put in back in 1961 was quite defective. Dr. Kirklin replaced that and put in an aortic homograft, which is a cadaver valve. A healthy aortic valve is harvested from a deceased person, preserved, and given to a recipient during open heart surgery. That valve lasted me from 1967 to 1979.

Unfortunately, while in surgery I had a massive embolus to the brain—a stroke—which left me with the entire left side of my body paralyzed.

I really was impaired in functions. I was blind for a while. As I regained my vision, I found I could not write my name and had to learn how to eat food with a fork, how to conduct myself in the bathroom. I was spatially disoriented, so I could not brush my teeth. Wanda was busy putting toothpaste on the toothbrush and running it around in my mouth. She had to help me put on my shirt and pants. Immediately I began therapy to learn basic functions. I practiced making model ships and airplanes to regain my manual dexterity. After a few months, I seemed to have regained most of my basic skills quite satisfactorily.

Oddly, and I guess I should say reassuringly, I did not lose my cognitive skills, and so I could continue in the practice, even after a while doing catheterizations. Still, the operations I'd had were taking their toll. I had wanted to become a heart surgeon but I was told that I should pursue a less vigorous lifestyle. I should take up my second choice: cardiology. So I stayed on the medical staff at the IU Medical Center, writing scientific papers, doing heart catheterizations and teaching doctors how to do clinical cardiology. The timing was perfect, as the field of cardiology was about to explode.

I was sitting at my desk at IU Med Center when an anesthesiologist from New Orleans knocked on the door. A leading hospital in New Orleans was looking for someone to set up a Department in Cardiology—an entirely new specialty. He wanted my wife and me to come to the Crescent City and look around. Naturally, at that time, we'd go anywhere anyone was offering a free trip, so off we went.

We were met at the plane by the recruiter-doctor and his wife, wined and dined in the French Quarter and put up in a plush hotel. On Monday I met with the hospital administrator, and I went through the usual interview questions and "getting to know you" and they called me back in.

"You're the seventeenth man we've interviewed," said the administrator. "The committee has decided you're the right man for the job." They would allow me to perform catheterizations, which I very much wanted. The opportunities were big. I waited for the mention of salary and it was far more than I ever expected to make!

Wanda and I were star-struck, but when we really looked around at New Orleans we weren't sure that was what we wanted as a homeplace for bringing up the children. "Thank you, but I will have to decline the offer," I said, and we returned home.

An interesting sidelight to that New Orleans story is that

the eighteenth man who was interviewed, after I turned them down, was Dr. Charles Steiner, and he took the New Orleans position and was very successful there. He became a very good friend over the next thirty years.

But I was never sorry that I turned it down. There's a right place for everyone, and things work out for you when you are in your right place.

The visit, however, had firmed up my desire to specialize in heart catheterizations. The diagnostic ability to determine patients' problems with heart catheterizations had been perfected to the point that I could think of this as a specialty of my practice: do it full time.

Dr. Edward Steinmetz, a former mentor of mine at the Indiana University Medical Center, who taught me how to do certain procedures when I was a fellow there, had decided to leave the Medical Center and go to St. Vincent Hospital. He asked me to join him. St. Vincent offered me a guaranteed salary of $35,000 a year. They wanted to build a heart program, and I guess they felt that I had something significant to contribute.

I would be on my own, so to speak, bringing patients into the hospital because of my own reputation and experience. They would pay for a secretary, office supplies, set up appointments and I would use their facilities and bill on my own.

It surely wasn't that lucrative New Orleans job, but it promised a bright future. I would be working with Dr. Harris B Shumacker, the famous heart surgeon, and we recruited Dr. John Isch, an excellent cardiovascular surgeon who had just completed his cardiovascular surgical residency. The years and opportunity ahead for all of us in this excellent hospital were boundless.

Heart disease was the number one killer of persons in America (as it still is) and now we stood on the verge of revolutionary changes. Something could really be done to improve the lot of hundreds of patients, and it could only get better.

I went to St. Vincent, with the proviso that I would limit

my practice to heart catheterizations. I remember one vascular surgeon on the staff approached me, probably thinking I didn't have enough to do, and said, "Bill, I want you to see this patient with high blood pressure. I looked at him and said, "You know, there's not an internal medicine doctor on this staff that couldn't do a better job of taking care of high blood pressure than I do." What I was really saying was "I want to limit my practice—it's really important to me." This particular doctor understood quite well, and continued to refer heart catheterization patients to me.

Initially I had two cases a day, then three, then four. Eventually when I had partners we did twenty to twenty-five heart catheterizations a day. I began generating an ever-widening practice. Most of my old referring contacts continued sending patients, with the circle in the state and beyond growing. Within three months the administrator from Community Hospital in Indianapolis was calling me, offering to double my salary to come with them.

I almost did, then Dr. John Isch met with me and said, "Bill, I'm a young guy. I came here for one reason only: to be with you. You are morally and ethically obligated to me to stay." Dr. Shumacker also strongly encouraged me to stay at St. Vincent. I discussed this with my wife, and she agreed. They were right, and so I stayed and have never regretted it.

In 1974, soon after I came, St. Vincent closed down the old early twentieth century landmark on Fall Creek Boulevard and moved to the expansive, well equipped hospital facility on 86th Street and Harcourt Road, going from three hundred beds to seven hundred. I look back at that old, red brick structure a little nostalgically now and then. As you passed through those light green halls you would see in a day's time almost every physician on the staff and give them a friendly "hello." That sort of intimacy can't be preserved in these new megahospitals, but, of course, there are other benefits.

The acquisition of the land for the new hospital was interesting. As northern Indianapolis grew, and along with that the necessity for a far Northside St. Vincent, several cornfields along Old Road 100 became for sale. The Daughters of Charity, who are the hospital owners, bought 100 acres, paying between $2,000 and $3,000 an acre. Truly, this must have been Divine guidance.

Several physicians, sensing the direction things were going and the need there would be for physicians' specialty offices, invested in land on Naab Road and on Harcourt Road. Today an area of several square blocks is a literal beehive of medical activity. That land is now worth $500,000 to a million dollars an acre.

We practiced the new specialty of catheterization in an organized way. If these people we were seeing were having chest pain, we proceeded by determining whether they were suffering from other sources than heart trouble: gallbladder stones, hiatus hernia, esophageal pain, problems with cervical spine and so forth. These needed to be ruled out. Then the patient could have a catheterization and if trouble was discovered, open heart surgery would be recommended if deemed appropriate. That was the remedy in the seventies for serious heart problems.

Meanwhile, cardiology was also slowly improving with the ability to diagnose and repair blockages in the coronary arteries. Coronary arteriograms would permit the diagnosis of these blockages. At the Cleveland Clinic by about 1967, the first coronary artery bypass was performed. Then Dr. Michael DeBakey, the famous heart surgeon from Houston, began doing this procedure and publishing information on his work. More and more surgeons became trained, including Dr. John Isch, who was working with us at St. Vincent Hospital.

Coronary angioplasty was not done locally until about 1981. Our group sent Dr. Cass Pinkerton to a meeting in Zurich, Switzerland, where he learned the technique of angioplasty from Dr. Andreas Gruentzig. This was a revolution in the treatment of heart disease. In 1981 Dr. Pinkerton returned to Indianapolis and did the first angioplasty at St. Vincent Hospital, and three or four years later stents came on the scene, and he started doing intra-coronary stents

We also became involved with pacemakers. Pacemaking technique had been known since the mid-1960s. Early pacemakers were primitive, but it was seen that they could reduce sudden cardiac deaths from complete heart-block (slow heart rate).

In the field of cardiology, we have seen the marked improvement of pacemakers with their lifesaving capacities, as well as improved technology in electrophysiologic studies, ventricular defibrillators and cardioverters. All of these things made a vast difference in the kind of work that we were doing.

But much of that was for the future. Our primary work in the 1970s with catheterizations was evolving rapidly. We did a right heart catheterization, a left heart catheterization, resting and exercise cardiac output and oxygen saturations, then cardio green dye curves. All of that took time—lots of it.

We soon adopted separate coronary artery catheterizations, debating among ourselves whether the Sones method (cutting down on the artery from the right or left arm to access coronary arteries) or the Judkins technique, (percutaneous right femoral artery approach) was the best, the safest. I chose the percutaneous femoral artery method (Judkins technique) and interestingly almost all the country does that now.

I practiced at St. Vincent Hospital with the original doctors I've mentioned, and others came also: Dr. Walter Jolly, Dr. Steve Fess, Dr. Stanley Hillis, Dr. Robert M. King. Later Dr. Mike Smith, Dr. Don Rothbaum and Dr. Joe Noble joined the team.

Dr. King took me to task for the work load, which I do admit was excessive, even for hard-working cardiologists. The first day he had full responsibility for covering for me was a Friday. As I took leave of him, getting into my car, closing the door, he said, "Bill, what is that flying up there?"

"Oh, I forgot to tell you, you have an emergency coming in by helicopter." He was up almost all weekend with that patient, and got a taste of what it was like. The patient, however, survived. That Fourth of July weekend was actually the first few days I'd taken off with my family in a long time.

Later, as Dr. King got the lay of the land, he complained, "Bill, you're killing me. I have a wife and children." We'd come to the hospital at 6:30 AM and we were there until midnight or even 2 AM. "I don't think I can take this pace."

I told this fine physician that if he would stay, I'd slow down the pace. But I tried, and I couldn't. I was just born to drive myself and others. Dr. King eventually went to Fort Wayne and developed the first cardiology group at Parkview Hospital, and he has remained a dear friend to this day.

And I did realize that recreation of some sort, time off, is a plus for a doctor. About this time I took Wanda and my children (by now another son Tony, had been added to the family) to the Four Winds Resort on Lake Monroe south of Bloomington, for a long weekend. We liked that resort style of living. Walking around with Teresa, Tom and Tony, I saw a man selling boats down at the dock. "You've got to have this thirty-two-foot Burns Craft houseboat," this smooth saleseman told me. It was appealing to think of having a houseboat with a little kitchen and ample sleeping space on comfortable beds for the family, with an upper fly bridge from which you could steer the boat. "Let's buy the boat," the kids urged. I did.

"Don't tell your mother," I warned the children. "We'll surprise her." So what did they do, of course, but run right in, yelling "Mom, guess what Daddy did, Daddy bought a boat." "We can't afford it," Wanda warned cautiously. "Well, I hope we can now," I ventured. It proved to be a wonderful recreation, and we did boating weekends for many years during the summer and for the thirty years that followed, though with some improved boats when the old ones wore out.

One incident I recall was when I was showing my old cronies from Terre Haute—Moffit, Britton, Sereno and Perrelle my eighteen foot ski boat at Lake Monroe. I slipped off and bumped my head and fell into the lake unconscious. None of my friends could swim. However, my good friend Dr. Ed Kourany jumped into the water with his clothes on, glasses and beeper in the pockets, and pulled me to the surface. Again, someone had saved my life and this time it was Ed Kourany.

And we were able to pay for the boat. Our cardiology department grew until we had to take out walls in the new St. Vincent to accommodate the growth of the cardiology practice. I'm sure that made some eyebrows raise among other physicians on the staff.

A few things fell through the cracks as we were carrying out all this intensive patient care. One of them was billing. I was supposed to do my own billing, and six months later, the hospital administrator asked me, under the subject of "How are you doing?" whether I was billing the insurance companies efficiently. Oops! Too busy practicing medicine. I guess many patients got the first six months' care gratis.

I had been working as a single practitioner. But by 1977 I wanted to expand and incorporate and take partners, continuing to work as a separate practice, but with St. Vincent Hospital.

I thought about the ideals I wanted for developing a practice. First on the list would be quality. It was imperative that we have the most modern medical techniques and equipment. Then, I wanted to test out the entrepreneurial—business and marketing—theories I'd enjoyed in the grocery business and apply their general principles to medical practice. See if medicine could be run as a good business. And, most of all to render patient care that was super—treating patients as people whom we cared about as individuals.

Who would join me as partners in the new corporation? Dr.

Michael Smith had been the first fellow in cardiology at St. Vincent. He trained with Dr. Steinmetz and me over a period of two years, in which he rotated through various services, learning about cardiac catheterizations, cardiology consultation and valvular disease. Dr. Smith joined me as the first partner. Dr. Cass Pinkerton, whom I've mentioned in terms of angioplasty, had trained in a fellowship along with Dr. Smith. The year Cass Pinkerton finished his fellowship, he joined us. We formed Nasser, Smith & Pinkerton Cardiology (NSP),which became official in 1978. Dr James VanTassel and Dr. Dennis Dickos soon came with us as partners.

In the meantime, Dr. Steinmetz, along with Dr. Stan Hillis and Dr. Donald Rothbaum, had formed their own cardiology practice, which came to be called Northside Cardiology. Was there competition between these two groups? Only a healthy, predictable amount, I think. Both practices were busy seeing patients. We respected each other as cardiologists and interacted socially as well.

In those early days we were jacks of all trades. One of us took hospital calls, one would work in the cath lab, one would work in the office. We did have someone to do medical records. Fulfilling the business goal I'd set for the practice, we kept generating new business.

Here's how we did that. When I left the IU Med Center after seven years on the medical faculty, I was pretty well known because I'd developed that system of state-wide referrals. I wrote all the physicians I'd come to know a letter telling them that I was doing a private practice in cardiology with the emphasis on clinical cardiac catheterization. They appreciated the personal contact, and began referring and encouraging their associates to refer also.

It was fun to be one of the first groups in Indiana to specialize in the private practice of catheterizations. It was also challenging to set up the practice the way we wanted it, and as always, personally demanding. I would get to the hospital at 7 AM. I checked the patients in the Coronary Care Unit or the acute Intensive Care Unit, taking care of their basic needs for the morning and letting them know their physician was personally interested. They'd had heart attacks, congestive heart failure or cardiac arrhythmias—rhythm disturbances.

At 7:30 I would start my heart catheterizations. We alternated with Dr. Steinmetz's group in the cath labs at St. Vincent weekdays. Heart catheterization procedures would go on until two in the afternoon, maybe later. Then we'd review the films and after that go up to the waiting room and tell the patients and families whether they needed medical management, heart surgery or angioplasty. At least that was an option after 1981. We were careful to spell out benefits and risks they would be taking if they opted for certain treatments and to take the time to listen to their questions.

Then back to the floors to see the patients I'd seen in the morning and on into Intensive Care. I made sure that I saw each patient at least once a day.

Many Indianapolis patients came, and referrals from Southern Indiana on a large scale, because there was nowhere for them to go between Indianapolis and Evansville. We were beginning to look like a real business venture.

But by 1979 I was in trouble again personally with my own heart valve. I returned to Birmingham again. "We were wondering when you'd be back," Dr. Kirklin said. "We knew you'd come eventually—most of our aortic homografts have not done well."

On that second valve surgery, a bubble of air had come into my system and traveled into to my brain, thus causing that embolism that deprived me of several months of active life. They didn't want to make that mistake on the third aortic valve replacement, so they laid out the red carpet. Dr. Kirklin put in a Bjork-Shiley mechanical aortic valve this time. The Bjork-Shiley intentionally doesn't close all the way, but allows a small leakage, leaving some aortic insufficiency in the valve. It worked better than earlier methods.

A third surgery for valve replacement can be of extended duration, because even though we keep advancing the technique, the third time around a surgeon has to deal with scar tissue from earlier surgeries and fibrosis. The surgery was skillfully done. I came through well and I still have that Bjork-Shiley valve. Each year I send Dr. Kirklin a gift at Christmas, remembering what he has done for my life.

Today I am the oldest living aortic heart valve recipient in the world—forty-two years.

I had not expected to buy a houseboat, but when my children insisted, I got it. The purchase was one of the best I ever made—a world of fun and camaraderie.

BLUE SHIELD
110 NORTH ILLINOIS STREET
INDIANAPOLIS, INDIANA 46204

1086042
20-1/712

TO
AMERICAN FLETCHER
NATIONAL BANK & TRUST CO.
INDIANAPOLIS, INDIANA

| DATE | MEMBER NAME | I.D. NUMBER | FILE NO. |
| --- | --- | --- | --- |
| 05-12-71 | BLUNK, IDA A | 009-09-7666 | 205788 |

TO THE ORDER OF:
NASSER, WILLIAM K MD
1100 W MICHIGAN
INDIANAPOLIS
INDIANA

PAY EXACTLY
$ ****.60

BLUE SHIELD MEDICARE SUPPLEMENTAL

This was my first check in 1971 from Blue Shield for my medical practice—sixty-cents, a springboard for future earnings.

WILLIAM K. NASSER, M. D.

ANNOUNCES THE RELOCATION OF HIS OFFICE

FOR THE PRACTICE OF

CARDIOLOGY AND CARDIAC CATHETERIZATION

AT

ST. VINCENT PROFESSIONAL BUILDING, SUITE 413

8402 HARCOURT ROAD

INDIANAPOLIS, INDIANA 46260

OFFICE HOURS
BY APPOINTMENT

TELEPHONE
257-9316
ANSWERED DAY OR NIGHT

It wasn't long before the expanding practice necessitated a new announcement and office.

Often the houseboat was the scene of happy night-time parties at Lake Monroe.

# A hero was needed and these 9 delivered

Heroes: you never know when they will be needed.

Nine heroes, who were there when they were needed, were presented with bronze plaques as they were inducted into the Red Cross Hall of Fame Wednesday.

Monty L. Anderson, 7205 Hatteras Avenue and the late Allen J. Pinkerton became heroes last June when they responded to the desperate pleas of Charles W. Harris as he was drowning in Eagle Creek Reservoir. He had fallen from the 56th Street causeway.

Anderson, Pinkerton, and James Harris, 3632 North Auburn Street, were enjoying a Father's Day picnic on the shore when they heard the cries for help. All three went to Charles Harris' aid.

The hysterical victim trapped James Harris under the water as he tried to use him as a lever to stay afloat. Anderson broke the victim's hold on the exhausted Harris and aided him during the 150-foot swim to shore.

**ANDERSON RETURNED** to the choppy water and towed Charles Harris to shore with the help of a towel.

*Anderson* *Comer*

After the victim was safely on the banks, Anderson returned to the water and attempted to find Pinkerton who had slipped below the surface. He was unsuccessful.

Heroism knows no age limits. Nine-year-old Ben Comer, Danville, became a hero on a cold day in January 1980. He and Darren Beck, 10, were returning from a day-long hike in Hendricks County when they decided to go sliding on the glassy ice of a pond.

Both youths panicked when the ice broke beneath them. Comer was able to leap to safety, but Beck fell into the icy water. Comer remembered his Cub Scout training and stretched a strong tree limb across the water to his friend. He then pulled young Beck to safety.

Everyone expects heroism from a policemen, but Indianapolis Patrolman Michael J. Rinehart went beyond the call of duty last September when he pulled Richard Baird from a burning auto on I-465 moments before the car exploded. Rinehart suffered burns and cuts on both hands during the rescue, but he continued to administer first aid until medical help arrived.

*Rinehart* *Nasser*

Tony Nasser, 5420 North Grandview Drive, refused to leave his father's side and kept him afloat for 16 hours after their boat sank off the shore of Marathon, Fla. last December.

**TONY AND HIS** father, Dr. William Nasser, and two other relatives were about six miles from the shoreline when the boat sank. The men swam together for an hour then the others swam ahead to get help.

Tony stayed with his father. When he noticed his father, who had had three heart operations, become delirious, Tony took off his life jacket and put it around his father. When Dr. Nasser lost consciousness ,Tony fought off his own muscle spasms and kept his father's head above water until they were rescued by the Coast Guard.

**DALE BEWLEY,** 255 South Bradley Avenue, was working at a construction site when he was beckoned to become a hero. He and another worker noticed that a nearby house was burning and rushed to see if anyone was trapped inside. At about the same time, Vernon Cox, 1419 East Marlowe Avenue, who lived near the flaming house, went to help.

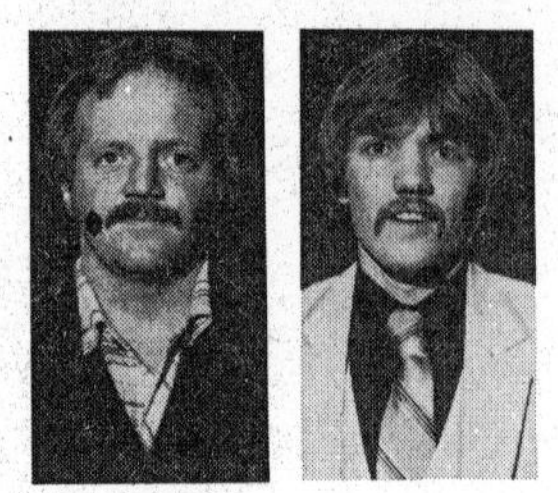

*Bewley* *Cox*

Cox kicked in the back door and heard Charlene Varney screaming for help. Bewley and Cox entered the house several times, but each time the heavy smoke forced them back outside.

On Bewley's fourth try he located Mrs. Varney, who was badly burned on the face, arms and legs, and both men carried her to safety.

Annie Crenshaw owes her life to the heroics of Donald Grover, 5607 Lunsford Drive, and Steve Hicks, 3442 Sherburne Circle. She was driving east on 38th Street last October when she lost control of her auto and the vehicle went into a lake at an apartment complex.

Hicks was watching televison in his apartment when he noticed the sinking car. Clad only in gym shorts, he dove into the cold water. Ms. Crenshaw, who could not swim, had rolled the car's window partway down when Hicks arrived and helped her through it.

*Grover* *Hicks*

**BUT THE HYSTERICAL** Ms. Crenshaw exhausted Hicks as she fought and struggled with him. Hicks called for help. Grover, who was watching the action from his car, plunged into the chilly waters and together the men managed to bring Ms. Crenshaw to shore safely. All three suffered exposure during the incident.

During its banquet at the Hyatt Regency Indianapolis, the Indianapolis Chapter of the American Red Cross is also presented heroism citations to the following persons:

Albert L. Alford, Mike Baskerville, Jack Cassaday, Daniel Clegg, Daniel Gammon, Michael Hill, John E. Johnson, Robert Keithley, Kenneth McCarty, Jack Morris, Oliver Pipkin, Chris A. Pitts, David Reel, Jay N. Reese, Thomas Remmetter, Douglas Reno, Lance Rutallie, Thomas Trackwell and Lorne W. Vandagrifft, all of Indianapolis, and Michael E. Kord, Beech Grove, and Denny Walls, Martinsville.

## Chapter Five

# We Beat the Sea

It was 1980. I'd had my third aortic valve replacement just twelve months before. Time was passing. My family was growing up. Teresa was twenty, Tom eighteen, Tony fifteen. I tried to take time away from the growing practice to enjoy life with them. After Christmas we went to Islamorada, Florida, in the Florida Keys. We took my nephew Billy Bob Radez, who is like a son to me.

Staying in the condo of a physician friend, Dr. Hussein Roushdi, of Community Hospital, we basked in the sun for a few days. Then, on December 31, the boys and I decided to do some scuba diving. Tom and Billy Bob and I had been PADI certified in scuba diving at Lake Monroe in Indiana, and we were eager to get in some more hours out by Tennessee Reef. Tony wasn't PADI certified, but he was probably the best diver of all of us.

I didn't think to tell Wanda and Teresa where we were going. It was a spur-of-the moment decision and like so many things in life, those sudden decisions can have lasting repercussions. In the case of those of us who went out on that boat, there were lifelong consequences.

It was New Year's Eve and the marinas we tried had already rented out their boats. Finally, at a small marina, we were able to pick up a sixteen footer with a 25 horsepower Evinrude motor. "That'll be extra for wet suits. Do you want 'em?" the marina man asked. It seemed like a lot of money for this small, sort of old boat and the wetsuits. We did take the wetsuits with us. We set our course for Tennessee Reef, which is seven miles from Islamorada on the Atlantic side.

The day was bright, the weather Christmas-sunny. We slipped over the side of the boat, went under the water, saw some barracudas and angel fish to our satisfaction and then surfaced. It was four o'clock and the waves were rising; apparently the weather had suddenly taken a turn for the worse. We got into the boat and pulled the starter cord to start back, with Billy Bob driving. Soon we saw the waves were so high they were breaking over the bow and into the boat.

The motor flooded out and the boat started sinking. The next white cap swamped the boat and we were suddenly left in the Atlantic Ocean with nothing but four life preservers and a duffel bag. Apparently the boat had no built-in flotation factors to keep it afloat, though we hadn't thought about that before. I thought of the barracudas we saw and wondered whether they really did attack people; the water was clear and only ten feet deep, but we were seven miles from shore.

We looked around. There was a flashing light marker not far off that we could swim to, but that didn't seem too promising. "Let's ditch our duffel bag and extra equipment and swim for shore," one of the boys said. We put the wallets inside the top of the wet suits Tom and Tony wore.

The four of us started out together. Soon the sun began to set, and as clouds streaked the orange colored sky, I shouted over to the others, "Isn't that the most beautiful sunset you've ever seen?" And Tony yelled back, "No, Dad, that's the worse sunset I've ever seen, because once the sun sets, it gets very black on the ocean." And that's what happened.

After a short time of moving forward through the dark, Tom yelled over at me, "Dad, you're still recovering from that surgery—I don't think you can swim to shore, can you? Billy Bob and I will swim for shore and send back help."

Tom, my oldest son and my nephew Billy Bob reluctantly

took leave of us, because they were the strongest swimmers and really our best hope for survival. "This is a matter of life and death," Tom said solemnly as he left, and stroked off strongly in the direction of the sunset.

Tony stayed with me. We continued swimming and joked a bit between ourselves, but we both knew the situation was every bit as serious as Tom had said. A front had come in; the winds blew hard and the air temperature was rapidly dropping—and so was the water temperature.

It seemed like an eternity that we swam on, water slapping at our faces, as we swallowed and stroked, finding welcome lobster buoys to hang onto for a few minutes, pressing on.

Hours passed. Where were Tom and Billy Bob? Had they reached shore? Found the Coast Guard? We didn't know, and I was growing dazed, worn out.

"I'm cold, Dad," Tony shouted over. He had a wet suit on, with gloves. I had only my Mae West life preserver. I wasn't feeling cold, probably because I was becoming hypothermic.

I couldn't see Tony, and he couldn't see me. Just two black heads bobbing in the Atlantic. At midnight, ahead, we saw fireworks. The town was celebrating, and distant sprays of yellow light bursts and red and blue trails lit up the sky. Hope dawned just a little. That was the shore, straight ahead, but it was still at least a mile off. And because the lobster buoy we were seeing was not getting closer as we kept swimming, not even staying parallel, Tony could tell that the current was carrying us farther out to sea.

Water splashed into my mouth with each wave which came towards us. My old, standard issue orange life jacket was waterlogged. "Tony, I can't make it," I shouted. "Swim for your life."

"Dad, I love you, and if we're goint to die, we will die together. I won't leave you." We held to each other, had a good cry, and then he pressed on, trying to decide how to keep his increasingly incoherent father, wearing a water-logged lifejacket, above water. Tony decided to keep me afloat by securing his own life preserver to me and getting rid of my defective one. "God, take me and let my father live," Tony says he prayed, and to my great wonder to this day, he meant it.

Meanwhile, Wanda and Teresa were frantic. We hadn't told them we'd be gone anywhere, and we hadn't returned to go out to dinner New Year's Eve. Where in the world were Dad and the boys? they fretted. Teresa was dating Tony Tanoos, whose father was the Assistant Police Chief in Terre Haute. She and Wanda called and asked Assistant Chief Tom Tanoos what they should do. The male members of the vacation party had not returned; it was getting late at night.

"I'll call the Coast Guard and they can start a search. They'll want to talk to you," he said.

By nine o'clock or so, the Marina owner had called the Coast Guard to say a small rented boat had not come back. The authorities didn't know who to call; the condo had an unlisted number, and anyway we weren't its owners.

At midnight the first break for the frantic, waiting family occurred when Billy Bob and Tom arrived on shore. Now that Assistant Police Chief Tanoos had established communication, the police and Coast Guard knew the condo number and called to say that two people had been pulled from the water and were at Fisherman's Hospital in nearby Marathon. No word on whether the other two were dead or alive.

We, of course, had taken the car and parked it at the marina, so there was no way for Wanda and Teresa to get to the hospital. My wife and daughter, feeling close to hysteria, begged a ride from a neighbor boy who was sitting with them, and they rushed to Fisherman's Hospital. Tom was on a gurney, extremely weak, so Wanda talked to Billy Bob. "Where are Uncle Bill and Tony?"

Billy Bob was weak, his voice hollow. "Aunt Wanda, I don't know where they are. They are out there somewhere." Later they would tell the story that two miles from shore, Tom couldn't go on, asking Billy Bob to piggyback him in. Later Tom said when he saw the *Titanic* movie, he understood how those poor souls in the jackets, floating near the lifeboats in all that icy darkness felt. You just fade out and fall asleep. Those last few miles, Billy Bob ferried his cousin, who held on to him in a "death grip" as he continued in his odd, crawling dog paddle with the life jackets for flotation. They, too, saw the lights of the fireworks, and when Billy Bob put his feet down, he touched sand. "Wake up, Tom," he called to the passenger he was towing in. "We're here and they're putting up fireworks to celebrate our arrival." Tom didn't answer. They headed more directly to the beach.

When they reached the shore, Tom was hypothermic, covered with jelly fish and totally exhausted and said, "Just leave me alone. I'm going to rest a minute." He lay his face down in the shallow water and Billy Bob had to drag him up onto the beach. At that point Billy Bob was worried for Tom's life—he was freezing cold and unconscious. He recalls trying to warm Tom up by burying him in a little pit, under a palm tree and covering him with beach pine needles and leaves. Then he told Tom, "I have to leave you now, Tom, to find help."

Billy Bob wandered up to the road and saw car lights coming. He determined to stand right in the middle of the road, hoping the car would stop before it hit him. A young couple took him to the sheriff's office: an ambulance was sent to the beach, where they found Tom up and staggering around, yelling at nobody and everybody. Billy Bob and Tom were taken to Fisherman's Hospital. Both boys were barely able to talk now, in the hospital, but Wanda didn't want to give up at this point.

"Out there—no!" she said. "We need to know where they are exactly. We'll go out and get them." She tried to find out more from Tom. "I just don't know where they are," he told her, struggling to find his voice. He raised his hand weakly and clenched his fist. "But I can tell you this. Dad is strong. They'll make it."

The doctors took over then, and Wanda and Teresa turned to talk to the authorities, who could not hold out much hope. They explained to Wanda that her husband and son Tony had been in the cold water a long time. It was pitch black. Their chances for survival were not good.

The Coast Guard began to search the black ocean. Teresa stayed with her brother Tom in the hospital; Wanda took Billy Bob back to the condo; there wasn't anything else to do but wait.

I have no memories of the last hours of that night. They said Tony put his life jacket on me and kept swimming around, hoping for rescue. We were about one mile from shore, but had drifted five miles south of our destination because of the tidal currents. The cold salt water had formed a film on my glasses; Tony took them off and put them inside his wet suit.

In desperation, there all alone, with his strength going and his legs cramping and the waves still splashing and the tide pushing us out farther, he prayed to God to give him the strength to get us through. "I can't do this alone," was his prayer.

Then, miraculously, he recounts that the waves grew calmer, the water seemed warmer, his strength returned and as he swam, the lights suddenly grew nearer.

The Coast Guard helicopters were overhead that night, but they could not see us, black heads floating on a black sea. When it grew light, a Coast Guard cutter spotted us and were delighted to see that Tony was waving, seemingly alive and fairly well. I was unconscious; they couldn't tell if I was alive or dead.

Someone leaned over the rail, looking at Tony from ten feet up. "Are you the Nassers?" the Coast Guard officer yelled. Tony told them we were, but he feared his dad had a stroke or was dead.

They lowered a gurney down into the water. Tony put me on the gurney, but the hook slipped as I was going into the boat, and I ended up back in the water. Tony re-tied me again and put me back on the gurney, and this time they were able to lift me, then Tony, into the boat.

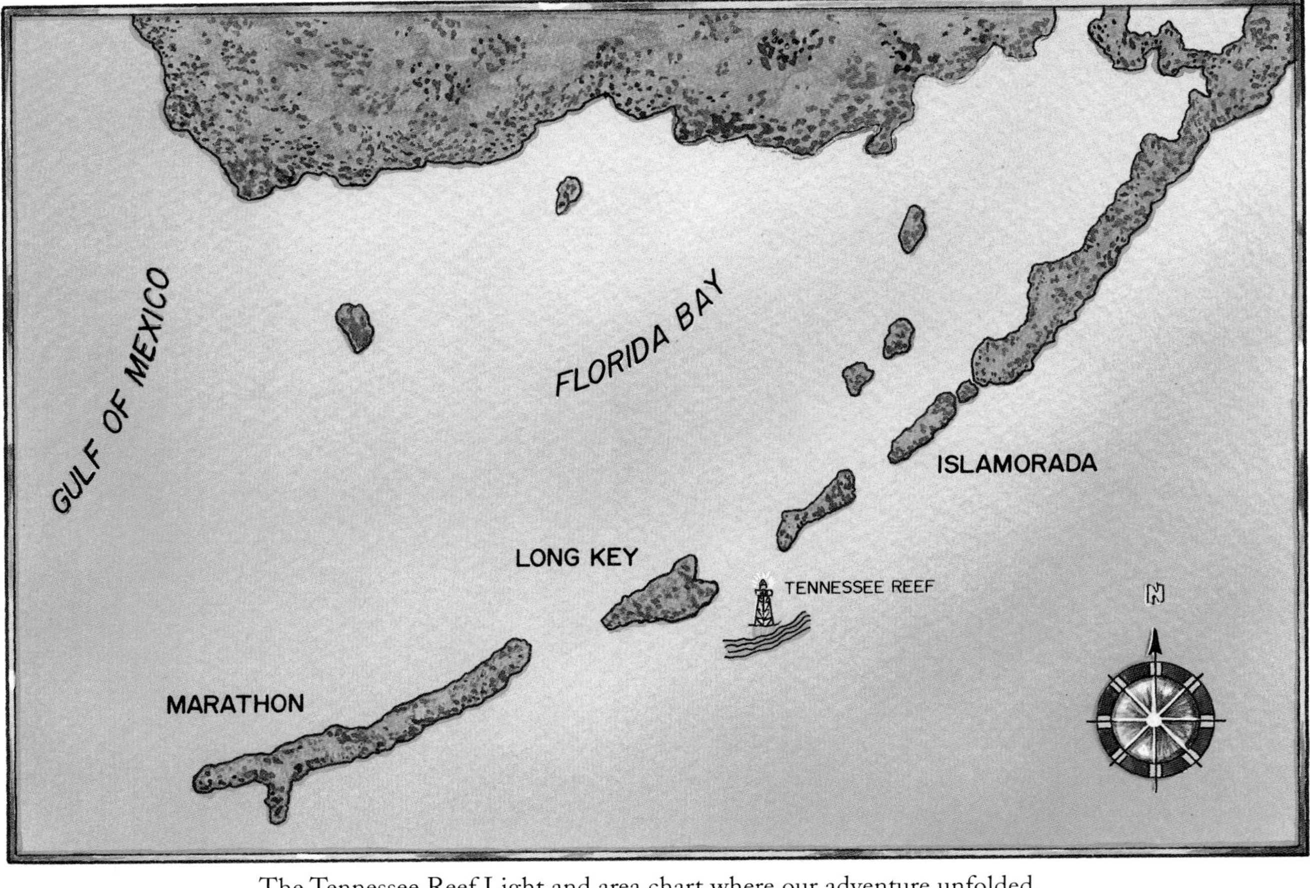


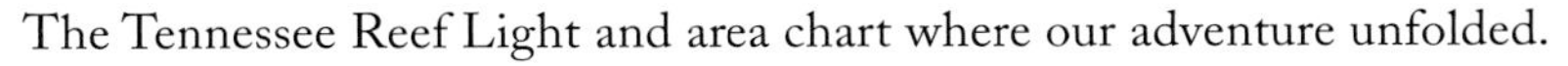
The Tennessee Reef Light and area chart where our adventure unfolded.

Tony and I share his “harvesting” before we start out on the ocean diving expedition.

We were glad to see the main causeway at Marathon, Florida behind us as we head towards Tennessee Reef for some open ocean scuba diving.

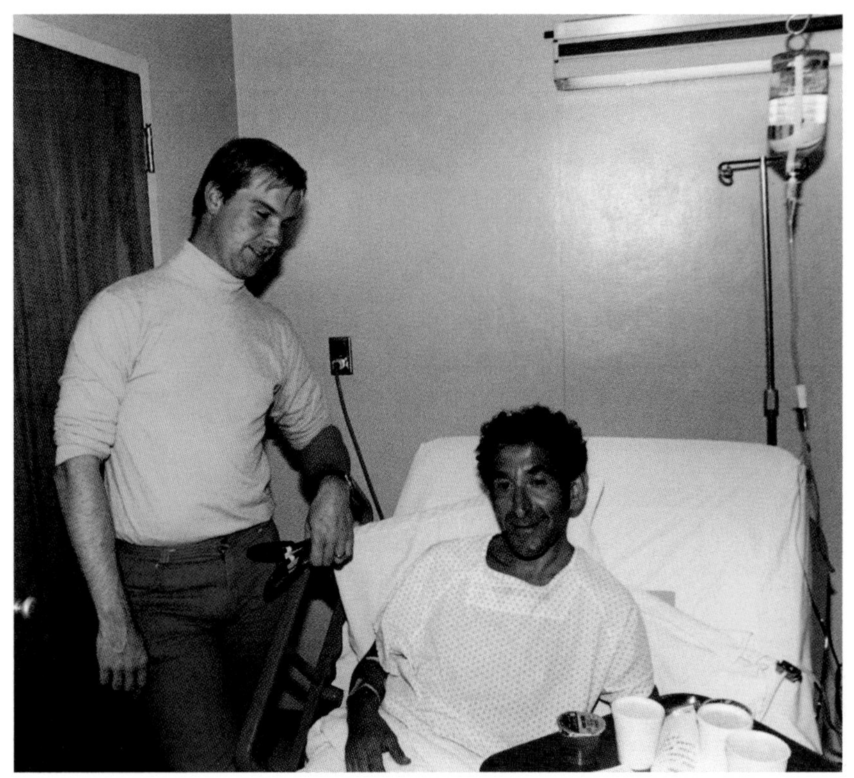

The attending physician at Fisherman's Hospital in Marathon confers with me, "The Survivor," January 1, 1981. Do I look like "death warmed over"?

Teresa giving thanks for the return of the ocean divers at the Catholic Church, Islamorada, Florida, Sunday, January 4, 1981.

Tony and I stand on the equator while touring Kenya on our African mission work.

I did have a pulse, and they could detect a heartbeat, although I was suffering from severe hypothermia. I was dusky and blue. They rushed me to shore where the Coast Guard cruiser docked at a pier. An ambulance was waiting to take me to Fisherman's Hospital in Marathon. So I'm told.

My first memory is waking up with lovely young ladies staring down at me. I was in a tub of circulating warm water; they were warming me up gradually. But my first thought was that these beautiful apparitions were angels, that I had died and gone to heaven.

My body temperature was eighty-seven degrees Farenheit, and my heart rate had slowed to approximately thirty beats per minute. I was turned into a sea animal, I guess, with a lower metabolism than human beings. I was bordering on death. My lungs were filled with sea water. I believe that if the waves had not calmed down before morning—a great spiritual gift, so Tony was able to have increased spiritual, physical and mental strength—we might not have made it.

There's a picture in Wanda's album of me in the hospital, wearing a hospital gown. In the photo I'm supposed to be "improving." My body temperature by that time has been raised, and the water was out of my lungs. But I look like "death warmed over," an apt phrase in my case at that moment.

But my billfold was there, with the American Express checks I always carry with me, two hundred dollars of good luck checks that I took to the hospital in 1961 when I had my first, risky open heart surgery. I hadn't gotten warmly dressed for the trip to scuba dive, but I'd had time to grab my billfold with the traveler's checks. They're always with me.

Four points to make:

(1) Tony was so little harmed by his sixteen-hour stint in the freezing water that he seemed to his mother and sister like he'd come home from a late-night party. He asked to go to Dairy Queen when they released him from the hospital and ate a ham-

burger and drank a strawberry milkshake.

(2) Billy Bob still cannot get over the fact that when the authorities arrived to help put Tom in the ambulance, the marina owner was also there to greet the exhausted swimmers. All he could say there in the dark on the beach in that dramatic moment was: "Where's my boat?" He claimed he had lost $3,000 worth of equipment. We declined to pursue the legal implications of his poorly equipped and unsafe boat. We were just glad to be alive.

(3) Billy Bob had saved Tom's life. He had hypothermia and had to be admitted to the hospital.

(4) Our son, Tony K. Nasser, won the American Red Cross Hero of the Year Award for what he did to save my life that stormy night off Islamorada in the Florida Keys.

Every New Year's Eve since, our family and a few friends, Ed and Carol Kourany, John and Zee Chalian and Mahfouz and Sylvia El Shahawy, have had a Survival Party. We go with our children and other family members on a New Year's Eve cruise in the Caribbean. Everybody goes out on the deck at midnight and we look at the stars and the ocean from the stern. We're wearing T-shirts that read "Survivor." We spit in the ocean. And we yell, "Neptune, you didn't get the best of us. We beat you!"

And Tom says the truth about how it feels for the four of us who lived through that ocean night:

"As we look over the edge of the deck to the ocean below us, we tell the story, and after we've offered a champagne toast to our survival, then we're quiet. I think we're all thanking God we're alive. It still can bring a tear to my eye. It must be imprinted forever in my long-term memory, and the remembered scene is full of emotion for me to this day."

The results were tangible in Tom's case. He became much more motivated in his education and focused on becoming a dentist, a Board certified endodontist (root canals) in private practice in Indianapolis. Billy Bob completed an MBA program and law school and is now a successful practicing attorney in Indianapolis.

And Tony says, "The incident changed my life. It reaffirmed my faith in God. It taught me for life that anyone can overcome adversity. All the struggles I had going through med school—I could face them. [He became a Board certified cardiologist with our group.] And today, when patients have difficult situations, I draw on that strength and energy gained that night. I firmly believed when that wind died that there was something left for me, my father and the others to do on this earth—some contribution to make. It was not yet our time to go, and I use that as motivation all the time. Nearly every day a patient reminds me of it, because many people seem to know about the incident at sea. 'Are you the one who saved your father's life?' someone will say. 'Well, yes I am,' I smile. And the story seems to give them something to feed on, too. Twenty-two years ago, but it is still keeping us all going."

# *Son saves father's life in rough seas*

MARATHON — Dr. William Nasser is alive today because of the efforts of his 15-year old son to save him from drowning in a 16-hour overnight ordeal in which the boy took off his own mae west and strapped it to his unconscious father.

The two were rescued by the Coast Guard Thursday morning after spending a harrowing New Year's eve floating in the Atlantic, battered by rough seas.

Dr. William K. Nasser, 43, of Indianapolis, Indiana, was listed in satisfactory condition today at Fisherman's Hospital after the 16 hour trial following the capsizing Wedesday afternoon of a rented 17-foot with four people aboard.

Nasser and his son Tony remained in the water overnight until their rescue at 8 a.m. Thursdav by a 41 foot Coast Guard boat. They were found about two miles off Duck Key, apparently having dreifted six to seven miles from where the boat capsized near the Tennessee reef.

Two of the men, Nasser's son, Tom, 19, and nephew, Bill Radez, 22, swam successfully to shore after the boat went down about 4 p.m. Wednesday, minutes after it started taking water. They didn't arrive until midnight.

The coast guard began the search .

The missing boat was reported at 6:20 p.m. on Wednesday by Fred Dawson of the Atlantis Marina, where the boat was rented.

The Coast Guard sent two boats out Wednesday night and a helicopter joined the search at 3 a.m. Thursday.

After the rescue, Nasser was taken by ambulance to Fisherman's Hospital in a state of unconscious shock. His temperature had dropped to 82 dgegrees from 98.6 and he was blue. Had it not been for the wetsuit top he was wearing, Nasser said, he doesn't think he would have made it alive.

"I said to Tony, 'go ahead and swim for your life because I'm not going to make it'."

His son refused to leave his father and stayed with him until he passed out from cold and exhaustion around 2 a.m. Thursday. Then Tony took off his own mae west and strapped it on to his father.

"He truly saved my life," Nasser said.

The current was powerful, Nasser said, "we'd swim 10 strokes and go back 20.

For Nasser's wife and daughter, it was the "worst New Year's Eve and the best New Year's day", they told Nasser.

## Chapter Six

# Medical Science and Increased Service Grow Together

It seems to me that after 1980 we were riding a wave. It was a wave impelled by the continually developing technology and medical science which meant improved health care for millions of Americans.

Finally, for the first time in human history those many, many of us who had problems with the most crucial organ of the human body, the heart, could look for improvement and even healing of their troubles through medical science and skill. We, and all the cardiology practices in Indiana, had our hands full trying to schedule all those who wanted care. We were pushed to constant expansion and increased efficiency and corporate management, and we welcomed it as a stimulating career and personal challenge.

In the 1980s Nasser, Smith & Pinkerton was working well, according to the practices we had set up. All the physicians who were hired were scheduled to become partners in five years. All partners were to make the same amount of money to the dime. I was the managing partner for the group, recognizing someone had to have the final word. Remembering those days, somebody recently called me the "benevolent dictator."

I kept remembering my original standards for the ideal medical group, and we kept pushing for quality. We developed the idea of a Center of Excellence. I guess it's a philosophical concept which means that all concerned work for absolute, sheer quality—the top. One can't go any higher, best of the best.

Care of the patients as human beings was all important, and

we had to figure out how to accomplish that with the more complex practice, with six or eight or twelve cardiologists involved. We developed a system of group assignments. In a given week, one physician would be doing catheterizations, one handling office calls, and one on call in the hospital. So a patient would see a member of our group, but not necessarily the doctor he or she had first met with or who had previously conducted a procedure. The patient saw a cardiologist from Nasser, Smith & Pinkerton, just not the same physician. But—if they were in the hospital, they saw that same physician for a week and got to know him. So there was continuity.

Patients weren't sure about seeing a group instead of one doctor, and although it was certainly more efficient and orderly, the old-fashioned GP in me, who had done all the hand-holding and baby-delivering in Martinsville, always had some reservations about this group care. Still, we had so many patients, and there were so many advantages to group practice.

We wanted to make the system as personal and error-free as we could. Obviously, we had to provide for twenty-four hour care. Someone was on duty at night at the hospital making late-night rounds. The information of the day duty doctor, who was assigned, for a full week, had to be communicated to the late-night rounds person, so that crucial information was passed on. But just as importantly, human details so patients could feel they were being personally taken care of. We'd have the physician on call that week with his nurse sitting down at a table with the night shift doctor and nurse, changing over with the diagnosis and treatment of each patient. Charts, or later computer sheets, would inform us of the patients, their diagnoses, their treatment and medications, who the referring physician was and so forth.

We'd say, "This patient has an acute myocardial infarction (a heart attack)." "This patient either has inferior or an anterior, is stable or unstable, blood pressure up or down." In most cases, actually, the daytime doctors were so familiar with the patients by this time that they could discuss the cases without the charts. Nurses filled out other details: when the patient was admitted, whether he or she was going to have surgery, angioplasty, medical management, when the patient was going to be discharged—all of that.

At six o'clock PM we'd do this change-over of about one-hundred hospital patients. By the end of the week we knew all of these people in the beds: their idiosyncrasies, charming and not-so-charming moments, as well as the medical history and status.

So then, if I were the late-night rounding physician, I'd go into all the rooms after the changeover and say, "Hi, I'm Dr. Nasser and I'm pleased you're doing so well. And I understand Dr. Jones, your physician, has been by." They were getting more than one cardiologist visit. We did try to personalize it, and they were pleased. Perhaps the reason I felt especially strong about this personal touch with the patient was that I had been a heart patient more than once. Surely that colored my view of how a patient should be treated. I remember lying there, in that cold metal bed, with the hospital gown on, bored and apprehensive. I remember how my spirits lifted when the physician came into the room, bringing confident optimism with him.

Different physicians contributed to the skill pool for the catheterizations, angioplasties, stents and eventually electrophysiology procedures. We could offer lots of specialization.

Part of the quality in our practice was being able to see a heart patient right away. Many people can't wait if they have serious heart trouble. I did most of the scheduling for referrals, and we admitted heart attack or other serious patients to the hospital the same day. Nobody needed to wait a long time for us. We had schedule "padding" which left room for some emergency or "right now" cases.

Since we were taking referrals, we had to have some way of continuing communication and care with a discharged hospital patient who was returning to Marion or Elkhart. We sent a letter to the referring physician detailing what had been done, diagnosis and continuing treatment recommendations on the day of discharge. Then the patient, who would be sitting around his family kitchen table after he'd returned from the hospital, realizing he couldn't answer his wife's and children's questions about the treatment he'd had or what the future held, could go to his referring physician, and that physician would tell him what we'd conveyed in the way of information. Everybody was in the loop.

The patient load by the mid-eighties was so large that we started sending some of our cardiologists to Community Hospital in Indianapolis in order to care for patients requiring hospitalization. The elective cardiac waiting list had grown to be as long as six weeks for heart catheterizations, which is just too long. There just wasn't room at St. Vincent. Eventually St. Vincent Hospital, my home base, began to object that we were taking away too much business, so Northside/Nasser, Smith & Pinkerton negotiated a contract which stipulated that we would be provided with more patient beds and could not go to other hospitals, but neither could St. Vincent hire any other cardiologists.

In the mid 1980s, with eight of us in the partnering group at Nasser, Smith & Pinkerton, as we'd be working with this distributive workload, we'd have one doctor in the cath lab, one doctor in the hospital, one in the office, and two possibly consulting. We averaged 110 to 120 in-patients in the hospital.

In 1986 the Indiana Heart Institute was formed. It was made up of Nasser, Smith & Pinkerton Cardiology, Northside Cardiology, Shumacker-Isch (the heart surgeons) and St. Vincent Hospital. We each owned 25 percent of the new entity.

It was a good step forward; we had been friendly rivals and now we were able to cooperate in planning and marketing. More importantly, perhaps, we could improve the contractual arrangements with third party payors because now we could offer a package price on heart care. We could provide patients with a heart catheterization, an angioplasty, a stent or bypass surgery, giving them a total package price. With so much focused power, we could give them discounted total care services and still be cost-effective.

The providing of information to both referring physicians and the public became a vital part of what we were doing. At the end of the 1980s we began offering seminars for physicians, Continuing Medical Education(CME), credit on special topics. "Women and Heart Disease" and "Update in Cardiology" were typical subjects.

As we headed for the 1990s, we concluded that consolidation was inevitable, and that this was bringing better care for all.

In 1987, as I was making ten o'clock hospital rounds, one of my former medical students, with whom I was good friends, a urologist now in private practice, met me in the hall and said, "Bill, I remember you were doing this in 1967 when I graduated from Medical School. And you're still doing it now."

I looked at him, then at my watch and said, "You're right. It's 10 PM and it is 1987, and I have been doing this for twenty years. And you know, I'm really being kind of overworked and my family—my wife and children—are being denied my presence." He stared at me, waiting. "You know, I have just made the decision," I went on. "At the end of this year, I'm not going to make late rounds any more." And that's exactly what I did.

And out of this new situation grew another innovation. Although I was no longer making late-night rounds, I kept up with patient records scrupulously, and continued to see the sickest cases. I took lists of all those who were discharged, and I was determined to contact all of the patients' referring physicians so the lines of communication would stay open.

I had a speed dialing system installed with the phone numbers of 200 of the most common referring physicians who sent patients to our group. So each day I'd take time to punch speed dial and let each physician know about a particular patient in that practice: whether they had had a successful angioplasty or what kind of medical management they needed, if any. The doctors—and patients—in Bloomington or South Bend, appreciated this new personal touch—seamless care.

Now, it wasn't unusual, of course, for cardiologists and other specialists to send information on the discharge of a patient. Usually that was done by the sending of a discharge summary. But if I were the referring physician in a small town in Indiana, I'd be glad to get a personal call, so I could ask questions and have the patient's situation fresh in my mind.

I did this because I wanted to maintain the chain of communications, but there were other benefits. I found that for every four physicians I would call, the group would experience a new referral from a doctor.

Of course, sometimes the patient died. If that happened—a trauma of course to everybody—I'd call the referring physician to tell him or her. If it was the middle of the night, sometimes I'd call right then or at least very early in the morning. I didn't want these doctors to hear from family members or the local newspapers that somebody had died under our care. I needed to share the details; I know I'd want to have that happen if I had a patient in desperate straits. Of course I knew many of these doctors because they came from the key pioneering referral towns that dated back to the IU Med Center days—Martinsville, Bloomington, Elkhart, Terre Haute. To them we had added Williamsport, Indiana, which was small but mighty in terms of sending patients from their entire area. Eventually the hospital there was called St. Vincent Williamsport.

All of this calling took up to three or four hours of my day, but my group believed this was the most valuable use of my time.

We were the first cardiology specialists in Indianapolis seeing patients in a group setting. At this time we also began hiring our own nurses to accompany us in the hospitals and transcriptionists to handle the large volume of medical records. By the end of the decade, we had put a particular stamp on the practice of cardiology and that was a group practice stamp. It would evolve further in the decade to come.

## Chapter Seven

# Combining Medicine and Entrepreneurialism

About 1980 I was asked to be on the Board of Directors at the Conseco Company, then in its first growth phase and being innovatively led by Steve Hilbert. As I sat on that board and years passed in the 1980s, I was aware of how these business people functioned: their command of financial projections and results, their constant analysis of cutting-edge methodology, and their use of technology. Especially interesting was their habit of buying other related corporations to expand their holdings. Of course for Conseco, that habit eventually went awry, but that was years in the future, and in the 1980s their habit of acquiring companies was farsighted and financially rewarding. I began to think about the methodology of business and to plan for the extension of the concept of entrepreneurship into medical practice.

Then, in 1990 we decided to hire a consultant, who could inform us what was the cutting edge for medical practices like ours. John Goodman and Associates in Las Vegas advised on cardiology practices only. They came to analyze the practice, to see how it compared with comparable ones in the nation, and to see if there was any room for improvement.

We had twelve cardiologists at that time, and we scheduled a night meeting with the consultants. Everybody plunged right in with too much talking and information-giving and question-raising. It was a disorganized melee. Afterwards, I literally had a headache. I said to John Goodman and his partner Conrad Vernon, "This discussion was so unstructured. I don't want to go through something like that again. Too many of us were pitching in. It's like this all the time—tough to make any decisions. Give me some suggestions."

John and Conrad nodded, then prepared a plan which included restructured decision-making. There was to be a board for our corporation, a decision-making body of only five of us, and the physicians in the corporation would rotate on and off the board. The board would be empowered to make all the decisions relating to policy. Each cardiologist from Nasser, Smith & Pinkerton functioning on the board in any given year would be chairman of a subcommittee which would investigate old and new methodologies and make recommendations for practice. One board member was chairman of the Finance Committee; another chairman of an Operations Committee. I was chairman of a new Marketing Committee. In addition there were Research and Strategic Planning committees. We were to meet monthly and report on findings and suggested actions for each of our areas of concern for the practice. Committees expanded after this time.

An in-house attorney was also hired, as a part of the new operations plan. Alan Dansker, an attorney with Bingham, Summers & Welch, had been my personal and corporate attorney, and now he would represent the practice. He moved his office to our location and was a full-time, in-house legal counsel.

Goodman said we needed an in-house administrator. Tom Steinmetz from Katz, Sapper and Miller accounting firm came with us full-time.

John and Conrad thought it would be a good idea if some of us from Nasser, Smith & Pinkerton would make some visits to successful cardiology practices which were using the board supervision system for their governance. We went to Wichita, Kansas and Ft. Myers, Florida, and shared information with their doctors and administrators. Goodman and Associates had national symposiums in Las Vegas that attracted cardiologists, heart surgeons and administrators. We spoke at those conventions, too, and got new ideas from others.

But that wasn't all that Goodman and Associates did for us. They plotted expansion of a major nature. Nothing can stand still; it was obvious that the demand for excellent cardiology services wasn't going to let us do that anyway. They recommended we go from twelve cardiologists to twenty-five in three years. Initially, this sounded unachievable. They specified the support personnel numbers and positions needed for that kind of expansion. They projected revenue and insisted we envision this sort of increased profit flow.

We enthusiastically endorsed their recommendations, and within only two years we had achieved the expansion goal, having reached a cardiology staff of twenty-five physicians, and all the support people, too.

In two more years we invited John Goodman and Conrad Vernon back to do another business plan for us. We trusted their know-how; they were consulting with other cardiology practices in Michigan, New York, Ohio and in the West and knew what were the successful strategies in practices in all of those places. We eventually became one of their largest cardiology groups in all the fifty states.

Lots of innovative things were happening in these practices, and the value of Goodman and Associates was that they could tell us what was and wasn't working. Many of the ideas we were hearing about were tempting, but John had an accounting background and Conrad had been in marketing and they were plenty savvy about directions the practices were going, so their crystal balls were clear and accurate.

For instance, they told us the Gatekeeper Model, a trendy charging system just coming in during the nineties, would not last. This costing method had each physician in a practice getting a certain dollar value per patient per month—capitation. It didn't last, so they were right.

They kept us abreast of insurance and managed care discussions, just then coming to the forefront. In the early Clinton administration, for example, cardiac physicians were being told that they would soon be doing fewer procedures because medical costs were going to need to be contained. Goodman and Associates told us that was ridiculous; Americans were getting older. They would be having the normal problems older people had with their hearts, so we needed to prepare for more services, not fewer. Again, they were clairvoyant.

As talk of managed care began to be on every talk show and medical newsletter in the country, we grew concerned about it. How would it affect us? John Goodman said it wouldn't—at least not very much. Indiana has Indianapolis and perhaps Fort Wayne, Evansville and South Bend as its big cities, but beyond that, many smaller rural towns with their own physicians referring to the bigger towns. Farmers and other rural patients from rural communities in the Hoosier state had their own private insurance or Medicare; they weren't going to be funded for health insurance by large, big-city companies. And that was good for us, because the small-town referrals to us were our "bread and butter."

In the nineties, twenty of the most prominent cardiology groups in the nation formed the Cardiac Leadership Alliance. These groups compared statistics and methods in such categories as revenues, production, patients seen, heart catheterizations, angioplasties, patients examined in the office , patients seen in the hospital and, most important—patient satisfaction.

I'm pleased that Nasser, Smith & Pinkerton usually led the stats in all of these categories. Whatever we were doing was working.

We were clearly participating in a wave of professional practice-building in cardiology that was going on all across the country, and Goodman and Associates helped us define that.

They'd told us what we were doing right and where we should go. But what about what we were doing wrong in the

A typical annual survival party held on a cruise boat on New Years Eve 1997. This was the 17th Annual Survival Party which includes: John and Zee Chalian, and family, Ed and Carol Kourany and family, Bill and Wanda Nasser and family.

Tom, Tony and Bill Nasser (l-r) visiting Tom at Newport, Rhode Island, during his endodontic training at Boston University.

Jan and Tom Nasser, William (B.T.) Tanoos, Anthony Tanoos (front l-r) Wanda and Bill Nasser, Teresa Nasser Tanoos, Tony K. Nasser (bk. l-r) at a St. Vincent Foundation Award's banquet.

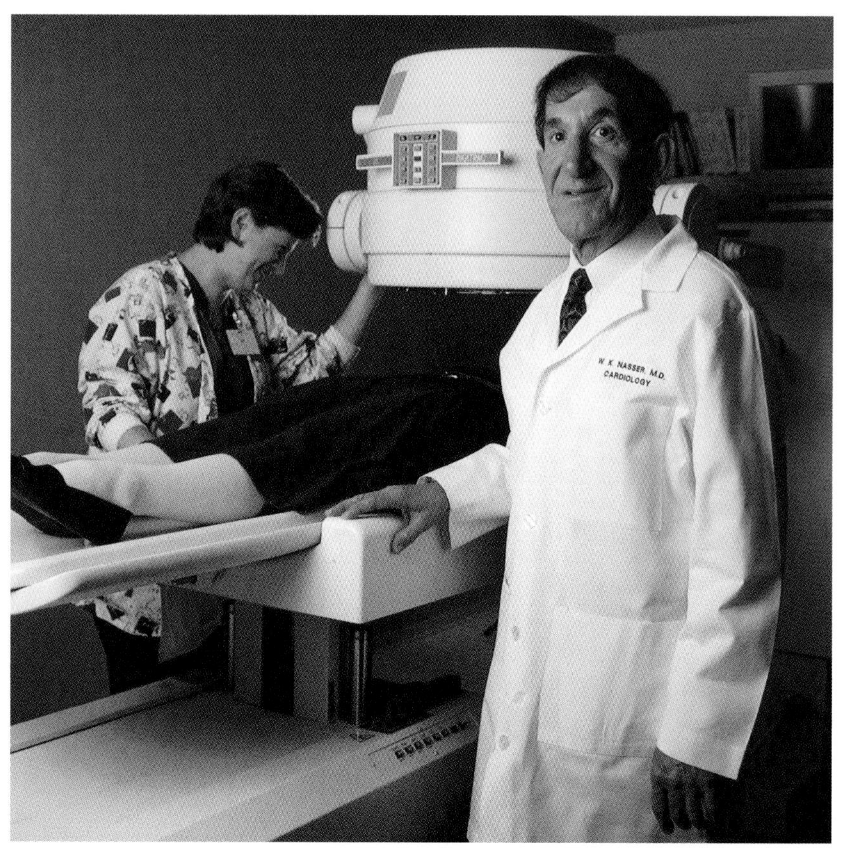


Photo courtesy of Shawn Spence.

The marketing brochure, typical of those we have used says:
"For twenty-five years, Nasser, Smith & Pinkerton Cardiology has been at the forefront of cardiac diagnosis, treatment and prevention. NSP self-supports ninety percent of its research, and has been a leader in numerous treatments including angioplasty, atherectomy, and intracoronary stents.
English novelist Aldous Huxley once said, 'Experience is not what happens to a man. It is what a man does with what happens to him.' Dr. William K. Nasser's life is proof of that statement—a fulfillment of the American Dream."

nineties? We were too lean. By that I mean that as they were monitoring our time spent with patients, testing frequency and timing, income and overhead, they found out that we were running an operation so lean that our overhead was only 27 percent. What's the matter with that? Well, it meant that physicians were doing too many nuts and bolts things—operational matters not related to seeing patients. We needed to hire more specialized personnel to do our records, scheduling, and insurance reporting and so forth, allowing cardiologists to see more patients.

We hired eleven new employees to do operational matters that first year the consultants were with us, and all of us generated more revenue. Among others, these were nurses who might know the Medicare coding so we could quickly process the unending bureaucratic records we had to work with each day. They performed efficiency studies; interestingly, these streamlined hiring practices did not increase the overhead.

How was routine, everyday procedure in the office being handled? How long were patients in the waiting room reading *People* magazine? Who took their medical histories and how long did that take? They wanted exact minutes to be monitored. How long did it take for them to get undressed and sit there freezing and impatient on the end of the examining table? Couldn't we reorganize our areas and allocate personnel and space so patients and doctors alike would have an efficient passthrough of the system?

They suggested, and we implemented, a separation of areas for patient workup. Diagnostic and clinical areas used to be mixed; soon we separated them. After the changes were in place, if a patient needed testing, he or she was off to another area which was not patient intensive but which could be accessed easily right at that time.

We were the first in Indiana to implement several other parts of innovative in-office patient management. We set up a group of schedulers who sat in the outer offices taking calls, listening to the descriptions of needs and then arranging for an office visit with a doctor. They knew the schedules of each doctor, the time needed for hospital duty and rounds and off-time and could put patients into the schedule on the basis of need and availability of the doctor's time.

Basic to the innovative office management plan was the concept of "one-stop shopping." Many practices, including ours in previous times, had patients come in, confer, and then come back later for a variety of tests, such as treadmill, nuclear testing and more. These tests might be administered on different days, and if the patient was an out-of-town referral, that meant returning to Indianapolis and taking additional time from work, inconveniencing both patient and family members.

With the one-stop shopping approach, the patient could be seen, worked up with the various tests required, and then have the results of the tests and plan for treatment given on the same day, in the same office. It was convenient for all concerned and alleviated patient worries that would sometimes stretch out over a period of days or even a couple of weeks.

We liked being first. You will recall that Dr. Cass Pinkerton did that first angioplasty in the state of Indiana and then the first stent. We had the first state-wide physician network. We did the first electronic medical records system.

Some members of our group were championing electronic medical records by about 1994. We hired a full-time information technology administrator named Roger Pinto, and one of his functions was the clinical services area. Roger had a good computer and electronic background, so he urged us to "go modern." Transfer all those thousands of old paper records to electronic format.

But how to do it? It was hundreds of person hours of work and took some know-how. We decided to have our physician's assistants, people who have had years of clinical cardiology training and are knowledgeable, transfer the old medical records to electronic data systems. We are a paperless system now.

At the end of the nineties, Roger had expanded the clinical electronic records function of The Care Group so substantially that he began to sell our system to other cardiology practices throughout the country. We began a new subsidiary to be called GEMMS, (Gateway Electronic Medical Management Systems). Although allied with NSP and Northside, and The Care Group, GEMMS has changed its location to capitalize on its success. Its wares are showcased at big cardiology conventions nationwide.

One of the most important concepts Goodman and Associates recommended was that we do just what I had seen Conseco doing: in our case, acquiring other medical practices to broaden our service network and revenue flow.

Of course our strategies were evolving as time went along and new challenges faced us. By the early-nineties it was obvious that other cities in Indiana were building first-class cardiology practices, and we weren't getting the automatic referrals we'd been receiving—really counting on. We were in danger of being "cannibalized," or, at least, starved.

What we needed to do was acquire cardiology practices in smaller cities in Indiana. Buy them out and have them join us—or send our cardiologists to the city to set up practices where there weren't any. In Kokomo, Terre Haute, Richmond and Anderson, we sent cardiologists three or four days a week.

In 1991 we sat down with two cardiologists, Drs. Prakash N. Joshi and Subodh D. Gupte, in Marion, our first real acquisition. We showed them how we could mutually benefit each other, and they joined us. Within a couple of years they were serving patients much more comprehensively and their income had tripled. Ten years later they have expanded into a very successful, five-member cardiology group.

We could set Marion up with treadmills and echoes and nuclear camera imaging machines they could not have afforded there otherwise. It afforded so much better care to these medium-sized towns in Indiana. We did central purchasing, which was efficient for all of us.

We went beyond cardiology to also acquire primary care physicians' practices in Terre Haute, Richmond, Marion, Brazil and Carmel. They would join our referral system and feed into our growing network.

Any significant medical practice must of necessity depend on its principal doctors' prestige and reputations to help it chart new courses. Name recognition and the character and personality behind that name are important in the medical profession. From the patient who wants to see "Nasser, Smith & Pinkerton" because he's heard of it, to the family care doctor who must refer a patient and wants a respected health care specialist, to the practice which is considering consolidating with you, the name counts.

In this connection, I have to credit two men for building Nasser, Smith & Pinkerton. Dr. Cass Pinkerton was known as a brilliant interventionalist with exceptional skills in angioplasty and stents, and we drew a lot of patients from Michigan, Kentucky, Illinois and Ohio because of him. And eventually patients flew in from Poland, Germany, England, Italy, France, and the Persian Gulf. Dr. Mike Smith was a "workhorse" who covered extra patient hours and night call when I was too sick to do so.

Eli Lilly & Co. developed Advanced Catheter Systems, which became the Guidant Corporation, specializing in medical devices. Ron Dollins, the president of that group, recognized Cass Pinkerton's talent immediately, and Cass joined Guidant's Advisory Board. Cass traveled, giving lectures, and we became known through him, too. He was the inventor of the Pinkerton catheter. He was probably the best cardiology technician I have ever seen. Watching him was like watching a symphony maestro directing an orchestra. We miss him today, but his dynamic spirit is still with us.

More recently our cardiologists have lectured internationally, going to China, Italy, Spain, Egypt, Germany, Turkey, Greece, Austria and Scandinavia on medical education cruises, where physicians obtain CME credits for continuing their medical education.

In 1995 we had patients coming from eighty-eight of the ninety-two counties in Indiana.

All this increased practice, of course, necessitated expansion of physical space. In 1974 I had begun my private practice in the original St. Vincent Professional Building—2,500 square feet on the fourth floor. As the need grew, we expanded on that floor until eventually we occupied the entire fourth floor and half the sixth floor.

We had long since outgrown that building, and so the Indiana Heart Institute Building was constructed in 1994 and we took over 45,000 square feet there on its fourth floor. Northside Cardiology had the second floor, and the heart surgeons and the Indiana Heart Institute had the third floor. So we were all together under one umbrella, but we maintained some sense of separate identities.

In 1999, the amalgamation of cardiac groups and services took the name of The Care Group, a merger of Nasser, Smith & Pinkerton Cardiology and Northside Cardiology at St. Vincent Hospital. Storer-Schmidt Cardiology at Methodist Hospital also joined the consolidation.

The group has followed a board pattern similar to what NSP had set up, with a managing partner.

By the time the building was completed, we had already outgrown that space. So we took various parts of the practice "off campus"—especially the growing financial and electronic records management part of the practice.

The Cardiac Leadership Alliance, which we joined in the nineties, grew from twenty members to twenty-seven as the decade progressed. We began meeting at least annually and became, in effect, each other's consultants. Data was pooled so we could compare how many catheterizations were done per quarter, how many angioplasties, how many bypass surgeries. And what is the overhead of an individual practice? It's important to know how other groups function: what works for them. Since the late 1990s The Care Group has been the largest practice in the Cardiac Leadership Alliance.

Today approximately ninety cardiologists practice in The Care Group, more than the Mayo Clinic or Cleveland Clinic. We have thirty-seven sites within the state of Indiana.

By 1999 I was ready to step down from active management of Nasser, Smith & Pinkerton. Reluctantly, I stopped seeing patients also. Complications were developing in my own medical situation, and I had to address them.

When I had my three open heart surgeries, I had had blood transfusions, sometimes massive in the earliest cases. Somehow, through one of those blood transfusions, I had acquired hepatitis C, and over the years it destroyed my liver. I was very ill. Doctors estimated my life expectancy at about two months and nothing was going to improve the situation except a liver transplant.

That surgery was being performed at the IU Med Center, but I was not a good candidate there. I was sixty-six years old and had had three major heart surgeries. Younger people with more years to live were going to get the few livers that came into that relatively new program. Even if I were a candidate, I would have had to wait years to get a liver. Dr. Larry Lumeng, Chief of Hepatology at the IU Med Center, arranged for my transfer to the Mayo Clinic in Jacksonville, Florida.

Surgeons from the Mayo Clinic in Rochester, Minnesota, had set up an excellent program in Jacksonville, and it seemed to my physicians that I might be able to receive a liver there. No promises, but there was a chance.

Without much firm faith that it was going to happen,

Wanda and I flew to Jacksonville and began to go through the testing program. "They won't take me," I thought. "I'm old and a heart patient." Still, after they worked me up for a week, Wanda and I met with the hepatologist, a wonderful man named Dr. James Spivey, and the surgeon, Dr. Jeffrey Speers. They told us they had accepted me for transplantation.

"Well, OK," I said, delighted. "We'll go back to Indianapolis and await your call when you have the liver."

"No," Dr. Spivey said, "we want you to stay here. Your waiting period begins now." They gave me a little beeper, a pager like you get in restaurants these days. We called Tony, Teresa and Tom and told them to be ready, it could be soon. That was Thursday, and we went out to dinner and slept at the motel. On Friday, on our way back to the motel after dinner, the beeper went off. Wanda was driving and with both our hearts pounding fast and furiously, she pushed the "pedal to the metal" and raced to the motel in record time.

We made an anxiety-laden phone call and were told that a liver was being harvested somewhere in Florida. We were told, "Please stand by and be ready to be at the hospital within the hour if this is a 'go.' We'll call back just as soon as we receive the word." I was the first on the donor list for my blood type if the organ was an acceptable match. I can't begin to tell you the tumultuous thoughts and emotions that Wanda and I were experiencing. I think we were both immersed in our own deep thoughts, and we had no conversation during that interminable wait.

Meanwhile, we made a quick call to our son Tony to alert our family and friends that we were waiting to see if the liver was acceptable. Our Indianapolis friends, Lew and LuAnn Derrickson, had offered their private jet to bring everyone to Jacksonville when the time came. We would call as soon as we heard from the hospital.

An hour or so later, the call came. "The liver was unacceptable," they said, "so you may as well go ahead and get some sleep." We made a second call to the family, informing them of this turn of events and promptly went to bed for the night—or so we thought.

About 2 AM that same night the phone rang again. This time the message was, "We have a liver. Get here within the hour." A young man had fallen off a balcony, and his relatives had left a healthy liver to the organ donor program.

It's a good thing we were already packed, because we were too shook up to put clothing in a suitcase at that moment. Once again, we called Tony to get our family to the airport and on their way to Jacksonville, as we were leaving immediately for the hospital. Our children Teresa, Tom and Tony along with Billy Bob, Ed and Carol Kourany and Lew and LuAnn Derrickson, all flew down and got in about 7 AM. We had a kind friend, Glenn Tappan, in Jacksonville who met their plane on the tarmac and quickly whisked them to the hospital.

Meanwhile, Wanda and I were sitting in the Emergency Room filling out paperwork, and then I was admitted to a private room. There was so much hustle and bustle of nurses and doctors and surgical equipment coming and going that it seemed as if it must be daytime, but it was only three or four in the morning.

Surgery was being intentionally held up as long as possible until everyone from Indianapolis arrived. The children and friends came in and there was a lot of tears, hugging and kissing and praying as the doctors watched our family and friends wish me well. Then it was time for that long road to the surgery room with my wife, children and nephew walking with me all the way to the door of the operating room.

Surgery began at 8 AM on Saturday, June 26, and the wait began, as it had for me several times before. I had been on the waiting list for thirty-six hours.

Time and time again I see God is watching over me, and us all. Usually it takes ten to twelve hours to do liver transplant surgery, but mine took only four hours, under the knife of an exceptionally skilled surgeon, Dr. Speers.

My family and friends were around my bed before I knew I'd even been operated on and I had no pain. In seven days I was discharged.

After that there was a succession of problems that kept me at that Mainstay Inn Suites and the Jacksonville Mayo Clinic for about two months. There was rejection of the liver, and my knee was inflamed and painful. After many tests the chairman of orthopedics came in to me and said, "We're going to operate on your knee."

"Wait a minute," I said. "Why?"

"Because you've got inflammation of the knee joint."

"No, I'm not going to have knee surgery. I've been around here too long already, and I'm too tired to go through all that. What else is there?"

There was further testing. They brought in a consultant specializing in rheumatology. He aspirated fluid from my right knee. He took the specimen to the lab and found out I had gout. I had the "King's Ill," named because so many kings, including George III, the English king during the American Revolution, had it. Ninety percent of gout attacks are in the toes, but mine was in the knee.

It wasn't the first time I had turned down orthopedic surgery. I fell on my boat once at Lake Monroe wrenching my knee and the orthopedic surgeon came up to me and said, "We need to operate."

"On who?" I wanted to know.

"On you." I shook my head and waved my hand, and said no. They put a cast on my knee and I did heart catheterizations the next day strapped right to the table so I could stand up.

Well, I stood up for what I wanted, and I've always been sympathetic to patients who did that, even if I thought they were wrong.

In Jacksonville they began steroid treatment for the gout, and I got better immediately. I continued to improve to the point that inflammation subsided and my knee returned to normal.

The Mayo Clinic, large-scale system that it is, did a good job with me, no doubt about that.

During the liver transplant experience I was made aware of the difficulties of long-distance medical care. You travel across the country, usually paying high prices for the airline ticket; you stay in a motel and have to eat, rent a car, do laundry. All of these things are expensive. Then, too, you lose the emotional support your local community provides. But I can't really complain—they did a fine job and my liver is in good shape to this day.

Mergers and acquisitions. Many large corporations have done them through the last few decades. Merging and acquiring is done to decrease overhead, focus and streamline buying power and eliminate a lot of the competitive repetition that doesn't serve the customers—patients in our case—well. But many companies have made mergers work, and I think we have done that in medicine with the growth of Nasser, Smith & Pinkerton to The Care Group, with all its associated practices.

You have to say, though, that merging medical practices is not just like merging media or insurance companies. Here's why: in large business corporations stockholders vote on company policy based on the amount of ownership they have in stock in that company. Physicians, on the other hand, are the owners of their practices and patients. Many are idealists; almost all are individualists. A physician believes he is the complete owner of his practice and his patients and wants a say in what is done.

It was easy in the old days. At Nasser, Smith & Pinkerton we all came with relatively clean slates and developed policy together. That policy was group practice. We did things as a group, from the heart catheterizations to hospital rounds. You came with us, you understood you would be part of a group culture.

When we merged with Northside Cardiology to become The Care Group, their practice was equal to ours in every way, but their methods were different. For example, our schedulers and secretaries were used to the NSP crew of doctors, and new ones came in with different personalities—and there were more of them to adjust to. It could be stressful to these office people to have all these personalities to sort out. We had a peer review committee to determine what the best way to do things would be. And if you have two separate cultures which have evolved differently—it's hard to merge them.

For example, a patient admitted to Nasser, Smith & Pinkerton knew the group would be caring for him or her. At Northside Cardiology, you were admitted to a particular cardiologist. Some patients might not like the way the new, unified group was performing. They did, or didn't like having a group come in. The physicians involved might wish to stand up for their own way of functioning. Now we have evolved a choice which works well; you can see your own patients in the hospital or you can have the group see the patients. As it turns out, most would rather see their own patients.

In early 2000, the two different practices, so strong in their own ways and independent in their ways of functioning, were beginning to feel comfortable with each other.

# St. Vincent cardiologists pioneer coronary stent

## PRACTICES CONTINUE HISTORY OF INVESTIGATIONAL PROCEDURES

**BY GRETA SHANKLE**
*IBJ REPORTER*

Doctors at St. Vincent Hospitals and Health Services are investigating a new device that eliminates the need for open-heart surgery in some cases.

The coronary stent is a wire coil, resembling the spring in a ballpoint pen, that is used to keep an artery open if it collapses after angioplasty—the balloon procedure used to open blocked arteries. Without the stent, patients would require a bypass operation.

St. Vincent was chosen by Bloomington-based Cook Inc., which developed the stent, as one of 20 sites across the country to test the device, said Susan Yoder, Cook public relations manager. The local procedures are being conducted by Nasser Smith & Pinkerton Cardiology Inc. and Northside Cardiology PC, two of the partners in the Indiana Heart Institute at St. Vincent.

Although the stent has not received final approval from the U.S. Food and Drug Administration, Nasser has already tested it in more than 300 cases, said the practice's founder, William K. Nasser.

The stent procedure passed the FDA's circulatory system device panel in May 1992, and Yoder said approval is expected anytime.

### AVOIDING SURGERY

When Larry Snyder, a retired postal worker from Richmond, had a heart attack, he was sent to St. Vincent for treatment.

As a patient of Nasser, Snyder had a stent permanently implanted in January 1990.

"It was a relief that they didn't have to do open-heart surgery," he said.

The stent is one of several techniques Nasser has pioneered with Northside through the Indiana Heart Institute.

"We cooperate on nearly all of the new interventional techniques, which benefits the entire institute as well as the patient population," said Northside cardiologist Thomas J. Linnemeier.

Shumaker Isch Jolly Fitzgerald Fess & Glasser MDs Inc. and St. Vincent's are also partners in the institute.

Nasser, who founded his practice 20 years ago, said the stent would only be necessary for about 5 percent of angioplasty patients, but even that percentage can save health care dollars and speed patients' recovery times.

The St. Vincent investigation site was chosen because of the number of interventional procedures conducted, providing a large sample for testing the device.

"My understanding is that because of the volume of the heart program here, we are often approached by manufacturers who are interested in having products evaluated when going through testing," said Steven Krakoff, marketing manager for the Indiana Heart Institute.

Last year, Nasser and Northside performed 7,500 diagnostic heart catheterizations and

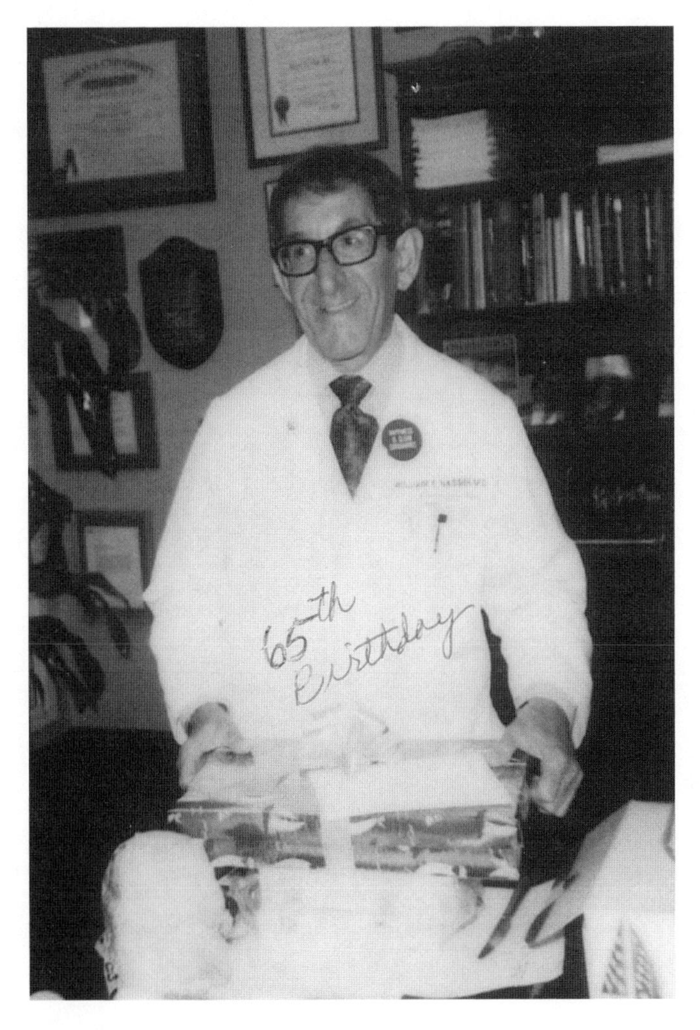


My 65th birthday—a celebration of a life.

## Chapter Eight

# Years of Fulfillment Giving Back to the Community

The Care Group has always wished to look five years and beyond to anticipate the heart care needs of the future. In the last decade I found myself becoming an apostle of change for cardiology. During the mid-nineties I presented data on new product development at international seminars. I told cardiologists at conferences and conventions about Cass Pinkerton's angioplasty and stent procedures. We did approximately 3,000 angioplasties in 1991, when that procedure was still under investigational protocol, and those who heard asked, "How could you do this? Angioplasty is still in research, and our hospitals won't let us do this because it can't be reimbursed." I explained that our hospital administration has always been visionary and supportive.

St. Vincent had its just reward. When angioplasty was approved by the FDA we were there, experienced, working already with many cases and ready to implement the system and get reimbursed. It was part of our goal of becoming a Center of Excellence.

We were, and are, involved in the testing of new medications and devices. A pharmaceutical company which is working on a certain cardiac innovation, either a medication or a device, will want to get certain best-recognized groups involved: Cleveland Clinic, Mayo Clinic, The Care Group at St. Vincent Hospital. The pharmaceutical companies make decisions about which hospitals will test their products.

In the recent past we have done research projects for manuscripts and for publication, too, and those hired with special talents along that line have added to that process. Dr. Bruce Waller is known nationally and internationally for cardiac pathology, and he has published numerous studies.

Between Nasser, Smith & Pinkerton and Northside—now The Care Group—considering an average recent year (1997), we've published approximately ninety major publications in international cardiology journals.

Research papers are usually presented at seminars and conventions, and we have been able to sponsor some of these events where our research was presented.

Lately, as the work of our Electrophysiology Department (EP) has become known, companies come to us to have patients test their defibrillators and the new pacemakers. Drs. Eric Prystowsky, David Rardon, Nancy Branyas and Richard Fogel developed our clinical Electrophysiology Department. We usually pick and choose among the companies seeking testing; so if Johnson and Johnson, Guidant or Medtronic and Cook come to us, our cardiologists can make intelligent decisions about which programs to test, based on their own knowledge and experience.

Also, we have recently received National Institutes of Health funding, as well as that of the St. Vincent Hospital Foundation. These activities add to our financial return, but they also build reputation and, naturally, they serve the overall good of excellent patient care-service to the community.

Of course, there is a lot of depersonalization involved with the growth we've had. It's inevitable. The Care Group has approximately 1,000 employees; the spur-of-the-moment evening dinners among friends and colleagues we had in the early days at St. Vincent are unlikely. Still, it's important to have staff get-togethers, and we all do so when we can.

Every decade will bring its challenges, of course, and its progress. Today The Care Group has eight female cardiologists. These women recently have been able to add a unique viewpoint to the understanding of female patients: they have been educating women in central Indiana on the need for preventative care of the heart. It has recently been discovered that as many women as men will develop heart disease. In fact, more women die of heart attacks annually than men.

It's also important to educate women because women make many of the health decisions in a family. Women often decide when it's time to see a doctor. Certainly it was that way with me all those years ago in med school with the night sweats, when Wanda told me to go see another doctor.

Our marketing, developed under the Goodman and Associates business plans decades ago, has expanded to respond to today's needs. Carol Kourany, who has led the marketing department for so long so well, developed the new emphasis on nutrition for heart health. She and her associates developed a program, Dining Å La Heart, which analyzed food items for caloric content, cholesterol, sodium and fat. Restaurants belonging to the program place a heart logo on their menus which highlights the "heart healthy" foods they were offering. Many restaurants in central Indiana signed on for this excellent health program. Another of Carol's ideas for "Dining Á La Heart" was a fund-raising event in cooperation with local restaurants to benefit programs related to heart problems.

And there's a tremendous amount of energy to be released for good in patient power. Those who have been helped with our cardiology services often believe they've experienced a miracle and would like to give back. Carol has organized the volunteer corps of former patients who help in the hospitals and the office.

I have continued to be loyal to IU School of Medicine, my alma mater. I'm on the Dean's Council and was especially pleased to be named IU School of Medicine Distinguished Alumnus in 1995. I tried to be helpful in the choosing of Dr. C. Craig Brater as new dean because I knew him well and believed he would take the institution forward, and I think I was helpful. He was Chairman of the Department of Medicine there, but I told him that he'd have to leave that behind and become dean if he really wanted to touch more lives. He should be a real asset for the program, which is aiming to be one of the top twenty medical schools in the country for research grants.

Recently the medical Class of 1961, led by Dr. Blake Waterhouse, raised money and created the William K. Nasser, MD Scholarship in Medicine, and it touched me deeply. Not only was that a fine recognition, but the needs for organizing the scholarship and awarding it has put me in touch with people from all the years I've been in practice: fellow students in medical school and students I taught. To have one's peers express gratitude and recognition for a life's work—it's incomparable. I told Wanda that night, "If I died tonight, my life's dreams have been fulfilled."

Sadly, as they were honoring me as a cardiologist, my own heart was having trouble of its own. I had an episode of syncope (passing out) just two hours before we went to the program. I was so tired. I fell to the floor. Wanda said, "We can't go."

"No, I want to go," I said. I took a thirty-minute nap, got up and got dressed and we went to that wonderful event. I ran across my own cardiologist there, Dr. Eric Williams. Wanda told him about what had happened, and he said. "I only want you to stay for a half hour or so. You shouldn't have come." But we did stay—until midnight.

In 1995 Tony and I had an opportunity to do medical missionary work in Kenya. We went with our close friends, Dr. Joe and Sarah Ellen Mamlin, as representatives of the IU School of Medicine. It was one of the most memorable experiences in my life. We saw poverty at the ultimate. This was truly a third world country. The health care budget of Kenya was approximately twenty-five million dollars and the population was approximately twenty-five million people. This provides an annual health care budget for each person of approximately $1 per year.

Diseases such as acute rheumatic fever, cardiomyopathy (primary disease of the heart muscle), typhoid fever and AIDS were rampant. Starvation, malaria and many diseases with which we have very little experience were witnessed by us. There were very few medical tools (i.e. electrocardiograms, x-rays, intravenous fluids, and so forth) that were available.

This made me very appreciative of my own health problems and care. I saw patients dying and yet no medical or surgical treatment was available to them. When I think of my own illnesses, being the recipient of three aortic valve heart procedures, a pacemaker-defibrillator and a liver transplant, it makes me very humble to acknowledge that I am in a country where these procedures are available and giving me a "second chance" for life. Again, we should appreciate the American Dream.

Nowadays I come to my office to process work for the St. Vincent Hospital Foundation, of which I'm the Chair of the Board of Directors. The foundation raises millions of dollars for the hospital system. Civic leaders and the CEOs of corporations in Indiana serve on the Board. The St. Vincent Hospital Foundation provides funds for medical research and education, equipment and facilities that keep this wonderful healthcare ministry on the cutting edge.

In addition, the charity work that is involved allows many underprivileged people to benefit both at home and abroad. Children from Bosnia and Haiti come to St. Vincent for free heart surgical procedures. The Indianapolis Unity Development Center, filled with needy children, has received a new van, televisions and VCRs, educational materials, free "fun days" and other needed amenities through the generosity of donors. The mission of the Daughters of Charity, now Ascension Health, is as real today as it was in 1633 in Paris, France, where it all began.

In my capacity with the Foundation, I have been able to utilize my resources of "Time, Treasure and Talent." I have been extremely fortunate to work with F. Duke Haddad, Ed.D. Vice President of Development, St Vincent Hospital and Executive Director of St. Vincent Hospitals and Health Services and Executive Director of the Foundation and meet his wife Cindy. Through Duke and foundation volunteers and donors, I've been able to open another chapter in my life—philanthropy—giving back to the community. This has enabled me to continue touching many lives, an extension of my passion through all these years.

And it has kept my perspective fresh. I've had the opportunity to work with great leaders such as the late James Kittle, Sr., who was past Chair of the St. Vincent Hospital Foundation. His wife Rhonda is a close and dear personal friend of mine who has followed her husband's lead on the St. Vincent Hospital Foundation Board. L. H. Bayley, a great civic leader in our community and past Chair of the Foundation, has also affected my life as a "role model." His wife Dianne has also been very active in the community and is a close personal friend.

Vincent C. Caponi, CEO of St. Vincent Health and interim president at St. Vincent Hospital, is an excellent leader at this great institution. St. Vincent is the "flagship" hospital in the Ascension Health National System, the largest Catholic not-for-profit healthcare system in the country. In the 2002 fiscal year, the hospital system was able to give to the community fifty-one million dollars in the form of charity care and community benefits. In addition, they provide free obstetrical deliveries for a significant number of sick/poor pregnant mothers.

Any comment about St. Vincent would be derelict without mentioning the work and vision of Sister Sharon Richardt, DC, who is Vice President of Mission Services. She sets an example for how we should follow the mission of Catholic Health Care. She represents the core values of the Daughters of Charity along with Sister Lucille Marie Beauchamp, DC, former Chair and Sister Mary Frances Lofton, DC, current Chair of the St. Vincent Hospital Board. They provide an inspiration to our past, present and fuure.

This organization recently added St. Vincent Children's Hospital to its list of services. The Children's Hospital is open twenty-four hours a day, seven days a week and provides emergency and trauma care to children throughout the state of Indiana. It is a futuristic facility which has the latest technological advances in health care delivery for pedicatric patients. The focus on this beautiful hospital includes pediatric oncology, pediatric intensive care, general pediatrics and the wonderful and unique Hilbert Pediatric Emergency Department. Dr. Harry Laws, a personal friend, has done an excellent job as administrator for this enterprise.

I'm in the office to advise on any Care Group matters that may be sent my way, to kibbitz with the secretaries the way I've always done and to talk to staff who drop in to talk about the good old days. Or the good *new* days. Cardiology is on the brink of even greater discoveries which will continue to revolutionize care of the heart.

The future can only see improved cardiology technology and skill and in the refinement of open heart surgery. We used to stop the heart, using a heart-lung machine, when open heart surgery was done. But now surgeons can operate on certain cases while the heart is still beating, and there's a marked decrease in mortality and morbidity with this new method.

In addition, new minimally invasive surgery allows the surgeon to make a small inch-and-a-half incision in the chest wall to perform valve replacements and coronary bypass procedures.

Many patients are benefiting from promising surgery and implantable stents. Cardiovascular physicians can now operate on the peripheral arteries in a procedure that lasts only an hour or two. They can insert a sleeve or stent into the aorta, femoral artery and other perirpheral arteries, with a catheter, to correct weakness.

New, promising thrombolytic agents (clotbusters) are decreasing blood clots which can cause trouble or death for patients.

And, the exciting field of molecular cardiology, a subspecialty of cardiology, to prevent heart disease is promising. The Human Genomic Project is completed now, allowing researchers to localize individual genes. One such promise molecular cardiology is bringing is the ability to identify the right drug dosage for an individual patient. This science is in its infancy but it is clearly a future direction for cardiovascular disease.

The Lilly Endowment has awarded Indiana University a $105 million grant for the Indiana Genomics Initiative.

As for my own heart, which has been through so much, it's still pumping. At the time of the liver transplant, a medication which was administered to me for rejection turned out to be somewhat toxic to my heart. But the performance of my heart is now aided by an intervenous infusion machine, delivering dobutamine, a cardiac inotrope,which makes my heart squeeze better. It's running all the time, fed by a battery powered pump. I'm on a blood thinner, and that function is monitored, too. I considered a heart transplant, but I wasn't a good candidate.

About seven years ago, I had two of those episodes of passing out (syncope), which usually results in sudden cardiac death. Fortunately, I woke up rather than died. As a result, a cardioverter-defibrillator was implanted in me. Just two years ago it was replaced at the Cleveland Clinic by the newest intervention called biventricular pacing, which paces both ventricles at the same time rather than singularly as in the past. Since the biventricular pacemaker was placed, I am no longer bedridden but am quite functional and enjoying a fruitful life.

I have concluded that cardiology's golden age is not over but is yet to come. Almost every major event in cardiology has taken place within the last three decades. It is all about helping people get better and eventually not need us. Lord Bryce, the English philosopher, stated, "Medicine is the only profession that incessantly strives to extinguish the reason for its own existence."

My family and friends still hold the survivors' parties on New Year's Eve. We'll keep on going, uniting with those who shared the experience, spitting in the ocean, putting on the T-shirts, as long as I can go up that gangplank. Southern Caribbean, western Caribbean, eastern Caribbean. It's the ocean we were headed to on that night. We fly out, we cruise together, we fly back together. We chant, "OK, Neptune, we cheated you!" But I don't drink any more, so the elaborate toasting is done without me.

I am particularly glad for the financial progress and stability in recent years that allowed The Care Group to have one of the largest and most profitable cardiology groups in the country. It confirmed my belief that quality medicine can combine well with true entrepreneurialism.

Entrepreneurialism is finding something you care about and enhancing it into the business of your dreams. I was doing that long ago when I was manager of my father's store and sold bacon as a loss leader to make "big profits." I explored it when I moonlighted as a young doctor, so I could test the limits of taking patients and caring for them efficiently. And as all the steps came, going out on my own, Nasser, Smith & Pinkerton, the Heart Center of Indiana and The Care Group, I tried to honor entrepreneurialism as a joint goal with dedicated patient care. Both can work together, and if both are done well, everyone benefits in society.

I guess I'm always combining business and medicine. I try always to integrate that mix with family life. I recall lecturing to the local Young President's Organization on their visit to St. Vincent about the business aspects of running a medical practice. You have to be a young CEO of a business of five million dollars or more a year to be in YPO. Just as they arrived, I was informed an acute heart attack patient was coming in from Marion. I asked the group if they'd like to watch, and they said yes. After asking the cardiologist for permission to watch the procedures, we all stood in the next room, looking through the window of the angioplasty suite and they all gaped open-mouthed at the angioplasty and the new stent procedure. Later some said it was one of the great experiences of their lives, an emotional experience, something to keep near to their hearts.

And near to my own heart was the moment when, to my surprise, in 1997 I was awarded the Indiana Entrepreneur of the Year Award. William McWhirter, Chairman of People's Bank in Indianapolis, had nominated me. Ernst and Young accounting firm has Entrepreneur of the Year Award dinners all over the country. I knew I was one of the three finalists, and it reminded me of the Academy Awards, sitting there in my tuxedo waiting to hear "the winners." And I can truly say, like those people who come to the microphone in Hollywood, that I did not expect to win. A spotlight shone on our table. It was a wonderful moment.

I think my dad would have been proud. He had accepted my decision to go into medicine, but in his heart he had cherished the hope that I'd have that supermarket with great weekly specials. I chose my own form of entrepreneurship. The recognition that Indianapolis people gave me at that dinner was particularly moving when I thought of the long road stretching from Terre Haute.

But another Terre Haute connection moved me even more, now, as I look back up the road from the poorer side of town in Terre Haute. As a young war veteran I'd committed to the life of a Catholic, and I'd never turned back. Those few moments on the rolling troop ship in the middle of the Pacific had changed my life, turned me towards the medicine which was my passion ever after that.

So I was touched when my sister, Beverly, brought a nun to see me, Sister Marie Kevin Tighe from St. Mary-of-the-Woods.

The nun said that realizing my health was slipping, they would pray for me. More than that, they hoped I would recover and become the second miracle for the Blessed Mother Theodore Guerín. In the early nineteenth century this remarkable woman came from France to Indiana to found The Sisters of Providence of St. Mary-of-the-Woods in Terre Haute, my hometown. She is a candidate for sainthood now, and they prayed I would be the second miracle attributed to Blessed Mother Theodore.

That was two years ago, and at that time I was so debilitated I couldn't walk down the hall. God and the biventricular pacemaker have made me better. Perhaps I'll be that miracle. But if not, I can only say that my whole life has seemed a miracle, and every moment I experience today still a continuing revelation of the joy of living. And, I hope, of serving my fellow men and women through medicine—and of cherishing family, friends and colleagues and former patients—each and every person that is near to my heart.

In spite of turbulent times, life has been good. When asked what I would change, if I had to do it all over again, I tell people, "I wouldn't change a thing, including my three heart operations, my stroke, our experience in the ocean and my liver transplant." They were all blessings in disguise. They afforded me the opportunity to bond with my family and with God and gave me a degree of empathy for my patients that I probably never would have had otherwise. All of them helped me understand what is truly near to my heart.